FRAGILE PATHS, STRONG HEARTS:
Stories of Rebirth

MEHMET AKPAK

AST PUBLISHING

BOOK EDITOR
MERYEM KELEBEK

TRANSLATORS
YOUSSEF HARVEY
RAIF B.
MERYEM KELEBEK

ENGLISH EDITORS
BARBARA W
HANDE HUR

ILLUSTRATIONS
MARIA STERN

COVER DESIGN
HAMZA YORULMAZ

PAGE DESIGN
MUHSIN NAZIF

AST PUBLISHING

FRAGILE PATHS, STRONG HEARTS: STORIES OF REBIRTH

www.silencedturkey.org
Published: July 2024
ISBN: 9798328225403

CONTENTS

We dedicate this work...

...to the tens of thousands of people in Turkey,
who have been deprived of their liberty and face persecution.

...to innocent people who had to flee their homeland and
get separated from their families.

...to all victims who have set out for a new life in which they
just want to live freely without any further injustice.

...and to those who have lost all their hope of going back
and living in their homelands.

We extend our heartfelt thanks to the narrators Farzona
Hazar, Aram Reman, Turkmen Hanim who sincerely share
their stories with us. Thanks to their honesty and sincerity, we
understand the past better and look to the future with hope.

We sincerely thank...

Our author Mehmet Akpak

Book Editor Meryem Kelebek

Translators Youssef Harvey, Raif B., Meryem Kelebek

English Editors Barbara W, Hande Hur

Illustrator Maria Stern

Cover Design Hamza Yorulmaz

...and everyone else who contributed to this project.

ABOUT THE
HIZMET MOVEMENT

Hizmet is a transnational civil society initiative that advocates for the ideals of human rights, equal opportunity, democracy, non-violence, and the emphatic acceptance of religious and cultural diversity. This widespread movement began in Turkey as a grassroots community in the 1970s in the context of social challenges being faced at the time: violent conflict among ideologically and politically driven youth, desperate economic conditions, and decades of a state-imposed ideology of discrimination that mandated a particular lifestyle.

Over the years, Hizmet has transformed from a grassroots community in Turkey to a wider global effort with participants from all walks of life. Their work is centered upon promoting philanthropy and community service, investing in education to cultivate virtuous individuals, organizing intercultural and interfaith dialogue events to promote more peaceful coexistence.

Hizmet participants are inspired by the ideas and example of Fethullah Gulen, a Muslim scholar who has expressed the belief that serving fellow humans is serving God.

For more information: *www.afsv.org*

EDITOR'S
NOTE

Advocates of Silenced Turkey (AST) is a non-governmental organization that runs its activities on a voluntary basis since 2018. The aim of AST is to bring before international public opinion the human rights violations including torture and the unlawful court trials and proceedings, which have been encountered in Turkey especially the last ten years. After 2016, more than 160,000 innocent people lost their jobs in both public and private sectors, with accusations and unjust convictions of being connected with the coup attempt. The state of emergency, which was announced on July 20, 2016, gave the government unchecked powers - in the disguise of combatting terrorism - to persecute thousands of people with no accountability and to undermine the fundamental principles of a democratic society and the most basic principles of universal human rights and values such as freedom of expression and freedom of the press. Today, tens of thousands of highly qualified professionals such as judges, prosecutors, doctors, teachers, journalists, academics, and military officers have been detained and imprisoned in Turkey due to bogus terrorism charges. Around 5,000 of them are women, along with nearly 345 children who stay with their mothers in prisons. Hundreds of thousands of people have little or no hope of surviving the grueling atmosphere in Turkey, and as they are banned from leaving the country, they have no other choice but to flee at the risk of losing their lives by crossing the borders via dangerous routes. Some of them have not survived this difficult journey.

As the Advocates of Silenced Turkey, we engage in a number of activities in order not to keep silent about the injustices that have been taking place in Turkey where the rule of law has been suspended for a long time.

APH (Archiving the Persecution of Hizmet Movement) project of recording and archiving the testimonies of victims, aims to shed light on the injustices suffered by thousands of people in Turkey. Our volunteers have conducted hundreds of interviews and thanks to their efforts, the victimizations, and hardships that the victims experienced are now being recorded in both spoken and written formats. The main purpose of this project is to ensure that these tragic stories are not allowed to fade into oblivion but are rather recorded accurately and impartially to leave firsthand sources for future generations. We also aim to bring this persecution to the attention of academics, media organizations, human rights associations, prominent community leaders, and government representatives at the international level.

"FRAGILE PATHS, STRONG HEARTS: STORIES OF REBIRTH" is the product of a long-term endeavor. Each of our works is a compilation of real-life stories encountered by victims whose true names and event details have not been revealed for the safety of their families in Turkey. We would like to thank everyone who made tireless and valuable contributions to this work. We wish that Turkey will soon transform into a democratic society in which fundamental values like universal human rights and the rule of law are duly observed.

The stories you will read below are based on real people and events...

I

FARZONA

as told by
Farzona Hazar

FOREWORD

Hello! I have come to you as a guest from far away. You have never been to my homeland, you might only have heard its name: Tajikistan. I bring the wildflowers that bloom on its mountains, and the cool winds that blow in its valleys. Although my name and country might seem unfamiliar to you, I am not a stranger to you. I am your sister, daughter, mother, teacher of your children. Soviet Russia had crushed and swept away my identity, culture, and religion. I have been looking for them everywhere, listening to the voices coming from the depths of my heart. In the loneliness of being an immigrant, I have pursued love and peace, not only for myself but for all the people of the world. I climbed the mountains of life, with a desire to see behind the surrounding clouds.

I was born in a land where we were made to forget who we were, why we spoke Tajik language, who our ancestors were, who our Creator was and how we could connect to Him by prayers. When I was a child, I knew only the name of my religion Islam, nothing else. The elderly around me didn't know anything about Islam themselves, how could they teach me something anyhow? All they wanted for me was to go to school and eventually get a job. My father was not around me, I had lost him very early. Those childhood years, full of sorrow and sadness, are now hidden behind foggy mountains.

I had to leave my homeland to silence the cries of my soul. Perhaps in some other lands, I could find peace and relieve the pain of my loneliness. A divine plan was guiding me. Praise be to God! Along the way, I have never forgotten my dear friends in Hizmet whom I have been blessed to meet. They have been the means to all the beautiful things I have experienced in my life. It is only a duty of fidelity and loyalty that I wrote this book.

My name is Farzona.

My Beloved **Dushanbe**

On a scorching August day in 1978, I was born in Dushanbe, the capital city of Tajikistan. Located in the heart of Central Asia, more than ninety percent of my country is covered by mountains. Dushanbe, too, is surrounded by mountains and hills placed so orderly as if drawn by pencil. Trees of all kinds decorate the foothills. Men walk around on the streets of my beloved Dushanbe, genuinely smiling with their eyes…young women wearing long embroidered dresses in bright colors, with cute toqi[1] caps on their heads. How can I forget the beautiful flower patterns on the dower chests of the brides? During the special holy days, you can knock on any door in the city; you would immediately get invited inside and offered delicious food. Even if the lights of all cities in the world were turned off, I would know my Dushanbe by its smell. The sound of the 4-string and 24-pitch rebabs[2] coming from all over the city is still in my ears. The saying is one of those rebabs in the city belonged to Rumi[3] himself.

Being a native of Dushanbe, using many idioms and proverbs of our rich oral and written culture in our daily language is not unusual. As a matter of fact, today I told one of my students one of those proverbs: "Not even forty different professions are enough for a

---

1 Toqi a short, rounded, and colorful skullcap, which is often worn for cultural or religious purposes in Tajikistan, by both women and men.

2 Rebab is a lute-like musical instrument. The body is carved out of a single piece of wood, with a head covering a hollow bowl which provides the sound-chamber. The bridge sits on the skin and is held in position by the tension of the strings.

3 Rumi is a 13th-century poet and Islamic scholar. He is widely known by the nickname Mawlana. Rumi's works were written mostly in Persian, but occasionally he also used Turkish and Arabic. His poems have been translated into many of the world's languages. Rumi's poetry mostly speaks of love which infuses the world.

man." I won't reveal now the details of why I told this to my student; however, one more time I have appreciated the ancestors who had coined this proverb, when I kept hearing the amazing stories of many brothers and sisters in Hizmet who were forced to migrate to many different parts of the world.

I've spent most of my life in different countries. Still, each mountain I see reminds me of my beloved Pamir[4] Mountains, and each dish reminds me of the sweet Sumanak[5]. In my early teenage years, I wanted to leave my city so much to go abroad. Alas! Now, I have a deep longing for the stone, the soil, the mountains, and the trees of my beloved country. Yet, it's not only Tajikistan which I dearly miss. There is one more country in my heart that I fell in love with and do long for. You will read my story in the following pages.

---

4 The Pamir Mountains, ranged between Central Asia and Pakistan, are among the world's highest mountains, reaching an elevation of 25,000 feet (7,620 meters).

5 Sumanak is a sweet paste made from germinated wheat and wheat flour, which is prepared in a large pot. The wheat is soaked and prepared for days. Traditionally, the final cooking would take from evening until the daylight and involve only women. They sit in a circle, sing songs, and have fun, each of them waiting for their turn to stir the sumanak. While stirring it, wishes are made. In the morning the warm sumanak is handed out to neighbors, relatives and friends.

That **Man**

My mother had gotten married while she was working as an accountant in Dushanbe. My father? I don't know. I have never wondered about him, either. Apparently, he had left my mom, our home, and our city when I was only one and a half years old. I have never asked anyone why he did so. I have never even held an imaginary conversation with him. The portrait of my father in my mind was colorless, odorless, and breathless in a vacuum for many years. During my life, I have witnessed many abandonments and separations similar to mine: the same lonely childhood years, deprived of a father's love and warmth. Whenever I hear of a divorce or abandonment, I find myself on a journey to my own childhood. I just touch and pass through the time period in which I have no memories with a man I have never seen. That man! The man who left us: Father!

After he left us, my dear mom tried to do her best to live an upright life by herself. After living for two years as a single mom, she wanted to give herself another chance and married another man. He was quite handsome but also quite untidy. He was fifteen years older than my mother. The house they shared was kind of like a shelter for my mom. For that man, however, it was only a place of resort. Because he was married to another woman at the same time.

So, this man, my stepfather, would stay a few days a week in the house that my mom and I used to stay and go to his other wife for some other days. Who was this other wife? How many children did she have? How did they live? Why did my mother accept this marriage? I did not force my mother to squeeze answers to these questions. I was three years old at the time. I had never seen my own father walking at home, never heard him knock on the door, never enjoyed time together with him at a dinner table. And yet, I started calling another man "father". I don't remember whether I ever hugged my stepfather. Hence there is no father smell that has permeated me. I don't remember when and how my mother made me say "father." In my memories, the word father and everything attributed to it were always far away from me. There was no one around me to bring me candies in his pocket, nobody whose legs I would hug, with whom I could share my troubles, and to whom I could act spoiled and coyly. Maybe that's why the word "father" has always been cold to me. Like a figment of imagination, in deserted places it melted and vanished like a piece of ice. What remained was only a figure whom I had seen a few days a week, shared the same living room and dinner table, and who gave me a few sentences of advice every now and then. A man, just a man…Ah! That word "father"! I wouldn't want to prolong this father topic at all, but I just couldn't help writing about it.

Tajik or **Russian?**

Speaking of fathers, there's also my grandfather. He had introduced my mother to a stepmother when my mother was only two. Just as I had grown as an unregistered child of a stepfather, my mother had grown under the care of a stepmother, who was actually of Armenian descent. It had occurred to me and stirred my curiosity only years later that her country was exceedingly far from my native Tajikistan. Yet more unanswered questions emerged: "When did she come to Tajikistan? What circumstances drove her to Dushanbe? How did she meet my grandfather and marry him?"

My grandfather signed me up for a private Russian school when I was seven. The admission to the school had required strong recommendations, which he had easily secured with his connections. The school's curriculum centered on music and social activities. I don't remember what I learned there or how, for that matter. Most of my teachers were Russian, with a few Tajiks among them.

I could only attend this school for a year; my grandmother and aunt had started to say that it was not right for me to go to that school. They feared that the Russian school would steal my childhood from me; that it would erode my Tajik identity with Russian customs. They kept saying that Tajik schools were in no way inferior, if not superior, to Russian schools. My mother eventually enrolled me in a Tajik school the next year. My grandfather accepted, although unwillingly. As a matter of fact, my mother, my grandfather, and my stepfather were all educated in Russian schools, learned Russian literature, memorized Russian songs, and were raised watching Russian films. This was probably why the Russian way of life had eclipsed Tajik culture in our daily lives.

As a result of this surrounding Russian culture, we were watching Russian TV channels every day. All kinds of alcoholic beverages were available at home, especially Russian brands. Everyone in my family identified themselves as Muslim, but it was just a label, nothing else. No one in the family would know even the word 'Bismillah[6]', let alone using it in daily life. Until I was twelve, I only knew how to utter some words of prayer. I was told that respecting my elders, cleaning their houses, or serving them while expecting nothing in return were ways to atone for my sins. Their kind words would pass as prayers, and I would be then protected from evil. The religion was reduced to a few words of prayer, that was it. I didn't know anything about salat [7], fasting, and other main prayer forms in Islam. We were

––––––––––––––––––––

6 Bismillah is a phrase in Arabic meaning "in the name of God" that occurs at the very start of the Quran and at the beginning of each chapter in it. It is one of the most important phrases in Islam and is used by Muslims mostly before starting "good deeds" as well as most daily actions, in order to receive blessing from God.

7 Salat is the Arabic term for the ritual prayer that is obligatory for Muslims to perform

Tajiks but were living like a Russian.

Azize

I was eight years old. My grandfather often used to tell us stories about the village where he was born and raised. On a weekend, we went to that village together. It was the first long journey of my life. We stayed two days in that village and saw everything that my grandfather talked about so many times: The roads, the cool weather, vineyards, vegetable gardens, all sorts of fruits. An old lady, in her seventies, hosted us at her house. I remember her name, it was Azize. Was she a relative of us, or just an old neighbor of my grandfather? I don't know. The night we arrived, she firmly grasped my arm and sat me down with her. When she asked me whether I knew some short prayers in Arabic, I said in all my innocence: "No, but I help my grandma and never upset my mom. Are these not enough?" She answered: "But darling, how can such a thing be? You must know the prayers of Elham[8] and Qulhuwallahu[9] by heart, so that you can

---

five times a day. Facing the qibla, the direction of the Kaaba in Mecca, Muslims pray first standing and later kneeling or sitting on the ground, reciting prescribed prayers and phrases from the Quran as they bow and prostrate themselves in between.

8 Fatiha is the first chapter of the Quran. It consists of 7 verses which are a prayer for guidance and mercy. Fatiha is recited in Muslim obligatory and voluntary prayers, known as salat. It is a powerful prayer in which Muslims invoke God's most beautiful names, attest to His sovereignty, seek His help and guidance and ask Him to shower His blessings upon them.

9 Ikhlas is the 112th chapter of the Quran which focuses on the unity and oneness of God. The complete translation is as follows:

"He is Allah, the One and Only;
Allah, the Eternal, Absolute;
He begetteth not, nor is He begotten;
And there is none like unto Him."

recite them whenever you want, wherever you are. You should recite them before you go to bed, or when you visit the graves of your past family members."

During those two days we stayed in that village, I had learned Elham and Qulhuwallahu by heart. After so many years, I was so surprised when I had learned that those prayers were actually some passages from the Quran. When we returned to our home, my grandfather gathered all the household and said, "Farzona will recite real prayers to you in Arabic, listen carefully." Whenever we had a guest in our house, he made me read those two surahs[10], he was so proud of me. Little did I know that I was reciting every single word of them wrong. I was just feeling so special. No matter how far our daily lives were from the Islamic way of life, reciting some prayers in their original form, albeit pronouncing them wrong, was a source of pride.

I Must **Leave**

When I was around thirteen years old, I was feeling as if the city of Dushanbe was squeezing the life out of me. I just wanted to run away from everything and everyone: the cold classrooms of the school, teachers who were so distant from me, classmates I couldn't associate with, and all the father figures around who were not there for me. Yet, my mom was hovering around me and doing her best to make me happy. She was so proud of my accomplishments, no matter how small they were. But my mom alone was not enough for me. My stepfather was coming to our house a few days a week but I was not having a meaningful interaction with him. He was just having

---

10 A surah is the equivalent of "chapter" in the Quran. There are 114 surahs in the Quran, each divided into verses. The surahs are of unequal length; the shortest surah (Kawthar) has only three verses while the longest (Baqara) contains 286 verses.

his meals and talking about some topics with my mom. He was providing some money for us, but it was far from being sufficient, so my mom was always working. I was feeling like a stranger in a foreign land…like a ship with no course, with no safe harbor around. I had to leave this place. I had to live in a foreign land, literally.

I was sitting with my mom in the kitchen when I said all of a sudden: "I want to leave this city." Quite surprised, she looked at me and said: "Is that so? And how do you think that would happen?" Well, at least she had not told me that she didn't want me to leave. Then she asked, "What is your goal?" I bowed my head, lowered my voice and whispered, "I just want to leave, Mom." I think she didn't disagree with my idea, since she lovingly caressed me with her eyes and said: "My dear, when the time comes, you'll leave. I don't think it is time, yet. But meanwhile what you can do is to go to the graveyard down the road in the neighborhood. There happens to be a special man's grave in there, he was kind of a holy man. Apparently, people who pray in front of his grave get their wishes granted. Go and pray there; and when the time comes, you can leave with his blessing." Mom said she herself was visiting his grave some days after work. She told me not to forget to wash my hands and face before I go there. That was called wudu[11]. She said that this is what one is supposed to do before a religious ritual. So did I. I walked around two kilometers to the graveyard. On the way, I imagined him: a very tall man with big hands, wearing a long green-blue clothing. His face was shining like the bright lamp in our house. When I was in the graveyard, I raised my hands and prayed silently but so earnestly. I didn't know his name. There were hundreds of graves around and I didn't know which one was his grave, either. I just prayed: "Dear holy man, who is here and whose name I do not know! I do not want to continue to

---

11 Wudu is the Islamic procedure for cleansing parts of the body, a type of ritual purification, or ablution. The 4 mandatory acts of wudu are: washing the face, the arms, wiping the head, and washing the feet. It is typically performed before prayers (salat).

live in Tajikistan anymore. I want to go far far away. Please hear my prayer and help me leave this place. Please!"

I didn't question at all what this man's power was, nor did I wonder how he would answer my prayer. I just prayed and prayed and prayed. For two years!

Road to **Turkey**

The Soviet Union had collapsed during the early 1990s. It was 1995 and like many of my friends, I had hopes of enrolling in the "Future Leaders Exchange Program" to go to America. Some friends were admitted to this program a year ago; those of us who stayed in Tajikistan envied them so much and said: "Wow, they are so lucky! They are in America now!" That year, I applied for the exchange program and took the admission exam. It was so unfortunate that I had fallen down the stairs in front of our house and injured my foot seriously right when I was supposed to take the third stage of the exam. I couldn't stand on my foot, let alone walk. So, I couldn't go to the interview and my plans to go to America had sunk. My mom and grandfather, seemingly sad, tried to comfort me. Most probably, they were happy that I would continue to stay with them. I, on the other hand, was sure that my prayers were to be accepted soon.

Two weeks later, a friend told me that it was possible to take another exam in order to be admitted to a university in Turkey with a full scholarship. She did, however, remind me not to get my hopes up because the exam probably wasn't too reputable. I didn't mind it and decided to try my luck. I was eagerly awaiting the results after I took the test. The long-awaited day came and I learned that I passed the test! My prayers were finally answered, I was so happy! My mom, on the other hand, didn't take it as well as I did. She was pregnant at the time and expecting the baby in a few months. She told me: "It is your decision, I leave it up to you. But I would rather you to stay here and help me with the new baby." And then she continued: "Didn't you want to be a medical doctor anyway? What is this nonsense of going to Turkey, all of a sudden?" How interesting it was that she had encouraged me to pray for two years long to leave here, and when I had a chance to do that, all of a sudden, she was acting as if she just hated the fact that I prayed.

Well, I was the only person around my mom who could help her. The baby she was pregnant with would be my half-sibling. I couldn't help but think that it seemed like someone else's child entirely. And she was right, I wanted to be a medical doctor, I had finished at the top of my high school.

As a result of my mom's heavy insistence, I took the exam to study medical school in Tajikistan. But the day I took the exam was also the deadline for me to submit some documents to the Turkish embassy. What did I do? I left the exam halfway through and rushed to the embassy to submit the documents. I didn't have the heart to tell mom what I did. When the exam results came back and she learned that I didn't pass it, she was quite surprised but she accepted it. Well, the road to Turkey was more open now. After a while, I received the news that all the paperwork for my journey to Turkey was completed. It was time! My mom couldn't object anymore. My stepfather didn't say a word. Well, my mom was making all the decisions around me anyway, it didn't matter what he had thought on this matter.

Izmir and **the Sea**

It was September of 1995. There were around three months left for my mom to give birth. Before I set off for the road to Turkey, I went to the graveyard on a Wednesday and prayed in the spiritual presence of that holy man whose name I didn't know. I pretty much touched every gravestone with respect and delivered the longest "thank you" speech of my life, under a gentle drizzle.

It was time. My stepfather had given me a small suitcase, which was only big enough for a few clothes of mine. To this day, I still remember how I hugged my mom and my grandfather. My stepfather gave me a few words of advice: "Take good care of yourself. You are our daughter. Don't forget that whatever you do in this life, comes somehow back to you." It was then that for the first time in my life I sincerely said: "Sure, Father. I'll take care of myself." He smiled and hugged me, although not with the same exuberance as my mom and grandfather. That smile and short but warm hug are the only sweet memories I had with him.

There were twenty-six more students my age. It was the first plane ride for almost all of us. We were so young; some of us cried along the way. I did not. Often times, I get emotional quite easily, but in that plane I did not cry at all. It was as if I had left my loneliness and sorrow somewhere else.

The Turkish embassy had arranged pretty much everything. Our destination was Izmir. There was no direct flight from Tajikistan to Izmir, so we had landed in Trabzon, from where we continued with a bus. The bus trip was just amazing: We passed beautiful green forests, the brilliant coast of the Black Sea, fog-laden mountaintops, lightened roads, colorful shopping centers and stores, and fish restaurants. We dipped in and out of cities, towns, and villages, each more beautiful and charming than the last. Cookies, cakes, and juice were served inside the bus every now and then. We also took a rest stop to enjoy a delicious meal.

They settled us in a dormitory in the Incirli district of Izmir. For the first time, I was living right next to the open sea with its own scent. When I first saw the sea, I compared its still waters to my quiet nature. It was as if sleeping peacefully like a baby in his cradle. Our dormitory was surrounded by palm trees. Each bedroom had its own bathroom. We felt so special to have been accommodated like this. We did not pay anything for travel expenses, tuition, dorm, or food. We were even given a stipend regularly.

The dorm was home to many students like us who came from other Central Asian countries. Some of them had arrived a year prior and so they helped us newcomers with the formalities that came with settling in a new country. In order for us to continue our university education, our Turkish language proficiency had to be at a high level. This is why we began attending the language classes held by TOMER[12], the Center for Teaching Turkish.

Early **Challenges**

Being from Tajikistan and other Turkic states in Central Asia, we were actually children of a culture in purgatory. At that time, I didn't know whether Izmir reflected the general Turkish lifestyle, but it was where we learned Turkish. We listened to Turkish, read in Turkish, sang in Turkish, watched movies in Turkish, and tried to speak Turkish like Turks did. Naturally, our way of dressing and

---

12 Abbreviation of the "Türkçe ve Yabancı Dil Araştırma ve Uygulama Merkezi" in Turkish, "Turkish and Foreign Languages Application and Research Center."

views on life were changing as well. Some of us started adapting to our surroundings very well. We were young adults who needed some discipline, guidance, and motivation. Sensing our need for direction, our seniors started relating their experiences to us. Apparently, many students who came from countries like Azerbaijan and Turkmenistan found Turkish easy to learn and left the language school to work as a translator in the famous Laleli district of Istanbul. Whereas earning twenty dollars a month in Central Asian countries was difficult, earning four hundred dollars in Laleli was easy and attractive. On the other hand, some students had serious troubles learning Turkish, eventually returning to their home countries. At the time, I couldn't understand why anyone would leave Turkey where there were so many opportunities to advance in life.

I ignored my friends' ebbs and flows, hesitations, and decisions they made for their lives and fully focused on learning Turkish. Of course, it was not easy. Actually the grammar structure of Turkish was very different from that of the Tajik language, but with hard work I was making significant progress. Working hard was also helping me to suppress my longing for my mom and hometown. The more time I spend studying, the less time I would have to think about other things. Back then, phone calls from Turkey to Tajikistan were quite expensive; I was paying around twenty dollars for a three-minute phone call. I had to wait also for my turn to make the call, for there was usually a line in front of the phone booth. My mom was calling me every Sunday. She was telling me how much she was missing me. She had given birth to her baby and my stepfather was staying with them more often. Half sibling, stepfather…I have never got used to these terms…like artificial flowers with no smell. I was forcing myself to fully accept them, but I just couldn't do it. They didn't mean too much to me. When I was leaving home, that man had looked me in the eyes like his own daughter. He had given me his own suitcase. I was not feeling too much for him, but I think I could consider the little baby as my brother.

I had promised my stepfather that I would take care of myself. So I was paying attention to each step I would take. I stayed away from youth groups that some friends joined and avoided talking to boys as much as possible.

Zulal

No matter how beautiful my room or the dorm were, I was still in a foreign country and lonely, after all. I would sometimes ask myself whether the prayer I had insistently made to leave my hometown was a mistake. Sure, now I was learning Turkish, but then what? Yet, I could've easily attended the medical school in Tajikistan with my mom being next to me. I even could visit my grandfather's village every now and then. And now? I had but a few friends. Some local Turkish students in the adjacent building were visiting us sometimes and asking if we needed anything.

One of those students was genuinely warm towards us, although she was wearing a hijab[13]. Why did I say "although?" Because my friend and I were comparing them to the famous Russian matryoshka dolls. When we talked among ourselves, we also referred to them as kapalushka. A set of matryoshka consists of a wooden woman figure, which separates at the middle, top from bottom, to reveal a smaller figure of the same sort inside, which has, in turn, another figure inside of it, and so on. The dolls are usually dressed in a long traditional Russian peasant dress. So, one of the local Turkish girls

---

13 Hijab in Arabic generally refers to various head coverings conventionally worn by most Muslim women. While a hijab can come in many forms, it often specifically refers to a headscarf, wrapped around the head, covering the neck, and ears but leaving the face visible.

who was dressed like a matryoshka was constantly visiting us. Her name was Zulal and she was a student in medical school. One day, Zulal told us that she and her friends were organizing a gathering to celebrate an upcoming Kandil[14] night. They would pray together and then eat together. What was this Kandil that she was talking about? Why pray on that night in particular? These were questions neither I nor my friends had answers to. Most of my friends didn't attend. But I did. I wanted to see how they were praying. It was in a local masjid[15] and inside was full of matryoshkas. It was the first time I had ever seen in my life that so many people were praying in congregation. Apparently, there were five holy nights that the Muslims in Turkey were celebrating. The one that we were celebrating that night was called Beraat Kandili [16], or "The Night of Acquittal." Zulal said that Beraat Kandili occurred on the fifteenth night of the month of Shaban[17]; and Beraat means to repent and to free ourselves of our past sins and start our lives anew with clean slates. That night, Zülal graciously and patiently guided me through my prayers.

---

14 Kandil refers to five Islamic holy nights, during which big mosques are brightly illuminated and the Muslim congregation recites special prayers. Special food dishes are often prepared at homes and shared with friends and neighbors.

15 Masjid in Arabic refers to mosques which are usually covered buildings but can be any place where prayers (salat) are performed, including outdoor courtyards. The masjid is not restricted to being a place of worship, a location for performing rituals, or a social dimension of the Muslim community. Instead, it serves as a symbol of belonging and identity.

16 Beraat Kandili is one of the five holy nights on the Muslim calendar. Devout followers of Islam believe that they should fast during the day until sunset. The night is spent in contemplation, reading Quran, and prayers, asking for forgiveness, purification, and salvation.

17 Shaban is the eighth month of the Islamic lunar calendar which begins its count from the Islamic New Year in which Prophet Muhammad (Peace be upon Him) and his followers migrated from Mecca to Medina in 622 AD, where they established the first Muslim community.

As the night progressed, I watched the other girls perform their prayers so seriously, and then embrace and congratulate each other so warmly. In that moment, I aspired to be like one of them. They were so devoted, sincere, and united. It is funny because in their sincerity and resemblance to one another, they were really like matryoshkas. They were completing each other, together as one they were so beautiful. That night, the smells, the sounds, and the sights of the city of Izmir didn't compare to what the masjid contained. The atmosphere in the masjid reminded me the peaceful moments I had when I was praying by myself in the graveyard back home. I was not feeling lonely anymore. I was together with all these beautiful matryoshkas who were praying for themselves and also for me. My deep loneliness was giving way to a new and strong hope. I could win the battle with myself. After that night, I never used those cynical words of matryoshka or kapalushka for those girls and stood against those around me who still did.

My bond with Zulal strengthened after that night. We saw each other more frequently. She was different; she seemed so wise for her age, and the way she spoke was truly calming me. On weekends and short school breaks, she would invite me to her family's house, which was close to the dorm. Their house was so big and she had her own room. But still, she was staying in a dorm room, together with other five girls. I didn't know why. It looked like she had a great relationship with her family, too. I was so glad that she was staying at the dorm since in time she became my best friend, my confidant, and in a way, my sister.

Each time I visited Zulal's home I was enjoying her mom's delicious food. I was staying in a guest room by myself. Zulal was always wearing a hijab and a light overcoat, but she never said anything against the way that I was dressing. She was constantly emphasizing the importance of inner peace and how one's clothes would change as seasons change.

Zulal eventually must have figured out that I didn't know the basics of Islam, so she taught me about religious and ethical topics. I wanted to learn more and more about prayers, wudu[18], ghusl[19], and many other things. Zulal would also occasionally take me to a private dorm where her friends were staying. That dorm was sparkling clean, and the girls who stayed there paid as much warm attention to me as Zulal did. We would eat together and then engage in thoughtful dialogues in the most fulfilling way. To make a long story short, my inner self was changing every day after meeting Zulal. It felt as if I had found a cherished treasure that I had lost a long time ago.

Hesitation

In 1996, after successfully completing the nine-month long Turkish language course, I took the college admission test which was offered to students who were not Turkish citizens. I was then admitted to the "Teaching Turkish" program at Gazi University in Ankara, which was the capital city of Turkey. Actually, I still don't know why I had chosen as my major "Teaching Turkish".

During those days, students from Central Asian countries had the opportunity to enroll in any two-year college program of their choice if they were already admitted to a four-year program. I was quite hesitant to have "Teaching Turkish" as my major, because I couldn't speak Turkish like native Turkish people could, let alone teach it; and what was I to do alone in Ankara anyhow? Meanwhile, it had been

---

18 See footnote 11 on page 18.

19 Ghusl is an Arabic term to the full-body ritual purification mandatory before the performance of various rituals and prayers. It is a full ablution or a ritual bath taken when in a state of major impurity to purify our bodies and ready ourselves to worship Allah.

nine months since I had left Tajikistan. I was repressing my longing for my mom and my hometown. When I realized that I was really getting homesick, I took the next plane in a few days and went back to Tajikistan. My mom was there at the airport to pick me up, together with Behnan, my baby brother. For a moment I couldn't recognize mom; she had lost so much weight. Later she told me that she had lost around 45 pounds. When I asked why, she told me that she had missed me so much after I had left nine months ago. "Every night I was crying and praying in the name of that holy man whose grave you used to pray by, for you to come back," she said to me. I was quite surprised to learn that she has been in so much depression, and this made me really upset. After a while, she began insisting again that I should stay in Tajikistan and study at the medicine school. Well, I took the test for med school and one month later the results were announced. My name was not on the list. Mom checked the list again and again, but in vain. One more time, she was so disappointed and didn't oppose my return to Turkey. So, I purchased the plane ticket and then went to the Directorate of Education to get some necessary paperwork. The official who was helping me with the paperwork asked me: "Are you sure you want to give up your right to attend the med school?" Totally shocked, I said: "But my name was not on the list!" He smiled and said: "You must've checked the wrong list. Since you finished high school with honors, your name was posted on a different list." Apparently, for all the checking and double-checking she'd done, my mom simply hadn't been able to find the list that had my name on it.

As I hurried home in a daze, I was faced with the biggest choice in my life so far: I was literally holding the admission documents to the med school in one hand. I had the plane ticket to Turkey in my other hand. As I explained the situation to mom, she got so happy but she left the decision to me: "At this point, it's totally up to you. Either you will take that plane or cancel the ticket." Mom was obviously all for me staying at home to study medicine and live with her. Actually, both of us had dreamed for a long time that I'd become a medical doctor. In that moment, if I had a scale to measure the weight of either path, I am sure they'd weigh exactly the same. If I somehow had two bodies, I'd send one of them to study in Turkey and the other one would stay here in my hometown. I didn't have much time to decide. I closed my eyes and tried to listen to my soul. For some reason, I felt that Turkey was calling to me. Yes, it would be nice to live with my mom and baby Behnan in my hometown. Being a doctor would be of high prestige, of course. They would address me as Doctor Farzona everywhere. But the question is: "Would I be really happy, really content?" The calling of Turkey, on the other hand, was so strong, loud, and clear. As if I could hear the voice of that holy man in that graveyard telling me: "Leave here, go to Turkey! There are so many like me over there, find them!" Of course, I had missed my dear friend Zulal and the other girls in Turkey, too. When I told mom that I wanted to leave to Turkey, she slightly bowed her head and began crying silently. Unable to bear the sight of my dear mother's tears, I left the room quickly.

Semra

After forty-five days in Tajikistan, I came back to Izmir. It was September 1996. I was still unsure of whether I wanted to study "Teaching Turkish." Earlier, I'd heard that Aldiyar, one of my Tajik friends, had been accepted into a two-year college program in the city of Edirne. As I mentioned above, the non-Turkish students had the opportunity to enroll any two-year college program of their choice, if they were already admitted to a four-year program. Thinking of my choices, I considered how I knew no one in Ankara, but I did in Edirne. Those days, modern banking system was being newly founded in Tajikistan; I thought it'd be better to study Banking and Finance to find a job back home instead of completing a four-year

"Teaching Turkish" major.

As I traveled to Edirne to start the enrollment process, I could only watch myself in disbelief. The old Farzona, the ambitious and decisive Farzona was gone. In her place was a new person who was just going with the flow. I could've been in the medical school's big lecture hall right now, dressed all in white. But then, Turkey was such a beautiful country, I was so lucky to live here. I think it would be better if I had stopped listening to myself and double-guessing my decisions.

The evenings in Izmir were no more, I had now greeted a new city. Wherever I looked, there were minarets[20] and domes. The Selimiye[21] Mosque, so delicate and elegant in its beauty, was just mesmerizing my soul. I had to do my best to deliver the sincerest, friendliest, and politest greeting to Edirne, lest I lose myself and drown in it instead. I completed all the paperwork for enrollment and began to stay in the dormitory. I was sharing a room with my friend Aldiyar. All I had in this city was that room, a bunk bed, and a desk in it.

Edirne was a smaller city than Izmir, but it still had a big-city atmosphere, especially for college students. Many Central Asian students tended to lose themselves in the nightlife of the city. Partying every night and alcohol abuse was considered quite normal. Pretty much, most students were following their desires and studying only a few days before an upcoming exam. My friend Aldiyar was the main reason why I had come to Edirne. Well, she had already made many

---

20 A minaret is a type of tower typically built into or adjacent to mosques. Minarets are generally used to project the Muslim call to prayer (adhan), but they also serve as landmarks and symbols of Islam's presence. They can have a variety of forms, from thick, short towers to soaring, pencil-thin spires.

21 The Selimiye Mosque is an Ottoman imperial mosque, which is located in the city of Edirne, Turkey. The mosque was commissioned by Sultan Selim II and was built by the imperial architect Mimar Sinan between 1568 and 1575. It was considered by Sinan to be his masterpiece and is one of the highest achievements of Islamic architecture as a whole and Ottoman architecture in particular.

new friends. She was not even staying in the dorm most of the time. One more time, I was in a deep loneliness.

I was quite selective when choosing friends. I remember one day back home, while having a meal together, my stepfather had told me: "Look at this slice of cake, Farzona. If someone were to eat it and leave some part of it, the other person wouldn't want to eat the leftover part. Not everyone can stomach a half-eaten cake." I don't remember whether I had completely understood what he meant then, but now it all made much more sense. Quite often, I was hearing stories of the girls staying in the dorm who had gotten pregnant. Then, they were buried in troubles that dwarfed any other existing school or life-related struggles. With self-preservation in mind, I closed myself off from my surroundings to refresh and replenish my soul. Often times, I was finding myself in the masjid of the dorm, it was like a refuge place for me. I was not performing salat five times a day but praying and talking to God in my mind was soothing my soul deeply. Tears in my eyes were accompanying my prayers. I was missing Izmir. I was missing Zulal so much.

One day, while I was sitting in the masjid of the dorm, again lost in thought, another student sat silently beside me and said hello. Her name was Semra. She was from the city of Konya. We sat together for quite a long time and talked. The way she talked and acted was so similar to that of Zulal. I wanted to ask her what took her so long to find me. I couldn't tell her how lonely I had been.

I met with Semra again later on. She invited me to a student house. The girls in the house were just like the ones in Izmir. We quickly bonded and I came to stay at their house a few nights of the week. They wouldn't let me do any housework, like cleaning or cooking. They were treating me so well as if I was a guest of honor for them. One more time I was bewildered by their unselfish acts and devotion. Just like at Zulal's house, I was feeling home again in this house. I knew in my heart that I could trust them, they were like my sisters. Their genuine smiles welcomed and warmed me like the softest of blankets. There were five of them staying in this house and they were all enrolled in the evening classes at the college. They didn't even need to wake up early, but they made sure to have breakfast ready for me every morning. Whenever they were cooking a fancy meal, they were always setting aside a plate for me and later on serving me when I would go to their house. Eventually, I thought, perhaps the reason I had come to Edirne was just to meet Semra and her friends.

My dorm room friend Aldiyar was living in her own world. One day she said that she was soon to be engaged and then having a party in a bar to celebrate. At our university campus beer festivals were organized, so it was not out of the ordinary at all to have an engagement party in a bar. I couldn't say no to her invitation. Since I wouldn't be able to enter the dormitory after midnight according to the rules, I told Semra that I would come to their house around 1 am that night.

Well, at the party, pretty much everyone drank alcohol and some of them got quite drunk. I was sitting in a corner and sipping cola. My family members in Tajikistan were regularly drinking alcohol, too, but I've never had a fondness for alcohol. Sitting in that corner and looking around, I had clearly understood, one more time, that bars and other sorts of nightlife were definitely not my thing, at all. It was 4 am when I finally got to Semra's house. Already embarrassed by arriving at such an absurd hour, I gave the door a timid knock. The girls opened the door almost immediately. Apparently, they hadn't even slept all night long. "Farzona," gasped one of them. "We got so worried, we almost went out to look for you." Well, at that moment, I said: "Why are you girls always like this? So much concern, and for nothing!" Then, instead of entering the house, I left and hung out with a friend of mine walking around for two hours, waiting for the door of our dorm to open.

It didn't take long, of course, for me to be ashamed of myself for that response I gave to Semra and her friends. After all they had done for me, in return for their unconditional love and care, how could I be so rude to them? At that moment, I compared them with Aldiyar, for whom I had moved into this city and who has been completely ignoring me recently. Semra and her friends were so worried for me all night long, while the "friend" from my hometown didn't care about me at all. It didn't take long for me to make up my mind, a few days later I gathered my personal belongings in the dorm room and went to the house where Semra was staying. When they opened the door, I told them "Can I please live here with you?" They hugged me with love and compassion. We were all crying.

Istanbul

In 1998, I completed the two-year program in the college. I was ranked second in my graduating class and following the suggestion of my friends, I moved from Edirne to Istanbul. I was admitted to the Department of Economics at Yıldız Technical University and got enrolled without hesitation. I was still considered an international student so I was supposed to stay in the dormitory but I decided to stay in a student house, similar to the one that I stayed in Edirne with Semra and other friends. Since I was fluent in Russian and Turkish, I had also found a part-time job as a translator within an international company.

Istanbul… you can only imagine how I felt when I moved from a small, calm city like Edirne to this huge metropolis connecting literally two continents. Fortunately, soon I made new friends like Zulal and Semra. Just as they cared for me, I was now caring for fellow international exchange students. Between all my obligations, I didn't even have time to feel lonely or homesick.

It didn't take long for me to discover the mosques and tombs of important historical and religious figures who lived in Istanbul. The tomb of Yahya Efendi[22], located in Besiktas, had the deepest impact on me. I went there pretty much every Sunday morning to conduct salat al-duha[23] and recite prayers thereafter. The main appeal of the tomb for me probably stemmed from how Yahya Efendi pleasantly greeted and conversed with soldiers on their way to a campaign from his tranquil tekke[24] during the time period of Ottoman Empire. This modest tomb became my primary sanctuary in this big city.

Praise God, I was also regularly performing my prayers five times a day now. I began learning how to read Quran in Arabic, this made me also study the meaning of Quran in Turkish. Hence my daily prayers meant more and more to me, with every passing day. These mosque and tomb visits, Quran studies, and taking care of my fellow friends had gradually increased my sense of belonging to Turkey. Most importantly, I fell in love with salat in Istanbul.

---

22 Yahya Efendi (1494 – 1570) is an Ottoman Islamic scholar, Sufi master, and poet buried in Besiktas, Istanbul. He served as a teacher of religious sciences during the reign of Sultan Suleiman the Magnificent. Yahya Efendi had close ties with the palace and consulted the Sultan throughout his life. After retirement, he built a dargah (see footnote 24 on page 39), numerous buildings and charitable trusts in Besiktas.

23 Salat al-Duha is an optional prayer to be performed any time after sunrise until midday when the sun reaches its zenith.

24 A tekke or dargah is a shrine or tomb built over the grave of a revered religious figure, often a Sufi saint. Tekke usually includes a mosque, some rooms, a religious school, and other buildings for community purposes.

My **Hijab**

I had lived that first year in Istanbul to the fullest. During the summer break, I wanted to go back to Tajikistan because I had missed my mom so much. That was the plan, but I was quite worried because I didn't know how they would welcome me. The thing is, I had begun to wear hijab some time ago like most of my close friends. It was not an easy decision, I had to find the answers of several questions first: Why should a woman wear a hijab? Is it very important to do that? How would my family react to it? I was feeling very content and happy with my decision. But I was worried about my family's reaction back home.

So, I went to Tajikistan with my hijab on. It was as if all my family members went into shock when they saw me with the hijab, especially my mom. "How can a young woman like you wear this thing? Where did this nonsense come from? Are you an old woman? How about you turn sixty and wear it then!" they cried in unison. During those years, young women who wear hijab were labeled as bigots, fanatics, and even uncivilized. Yet, I hadn't expected such a vocal response from my own family. Praying salat five times a day, once revealed, also became a target of criticism. When I was trying to focus on my salat, they were deliberately prodding and even pushing me around with their hands; not a single moment of prayer passed in peace. The tirades didn't end either: "Why is this taking so long? What is this nonsense, anyhow? Are you losing your mind? Are you an Afghan? A Pakistani? You'll pray when you're old!" I wanted to scream in response, but it wouldn't have helped. What I could only do was to try to find a place where no one was present to perform my salat. My mother, who had lost 45 pounds in one year because she had missed me so much, gradually increased her opposition to my expression of religion. She was constantly yelling and insulting me. At some point, it was unbearable anymore so I had to take my hijab out helplessly. There was no peace for me there anymore, I wanted to return to Turkey as soon as possible. I still had thirteen days of vacation when I boarded the flight back to Turkey.

In a cruel twist of irony, a bad surprise was waiting for me in Turkey. It was 1999, and the Council of Higher Education had banned wearing hijab in all the universities. Students were literally turned away from the university gates, they were only allowed if they would take their hijabs out. Apparently, there was no peace for me anywhere. I was only a poor foreigner in Turkey, nobody would care about my rights, really. But how about those tens of thousands of local Turkish girls who wanted to attend the college with hijab? This was their motherland! It was such as shame that they were treated so ruthlessly by their own government in their own homeland. Was this not the land of Yahya Efendi and many others like him? I had found peace here, I was happy with my salat, hijab, and prayers. But now there was a big wall surrounding me and I was just another brick in that wall of banned people.

I loved this country so much, even beyond its greatest poets. My lifetime prayers were accepted here. I was in love with its cities, folk songs, mosques, and adhan[25]. Now that love was smothered by dark clouds that desaturated the once-vibrant Istanbul. Everything looked gray all of a sudden, not even the regal navy blue of the Bosporus[26] could withstand the encroaching darkness. Protests of the students and the police intervention every day had tired me half to death.

What happened next? Well, unfortunately, many students had no

---

25 Adhan, Arabic, is the Islamic call to prayer recited at prescribed times of the day, summoning Muslims for obligatory prayer.

26 Bosphorus Strait is a natural strait and an internationally significant waterway located in Istanbul that connects the Black Sea to the Sea of Marmara. It forms part of the continental boundary between Asia and Europe. It is the world's narrowest strait used for international navigation.

other choice but taking their hijabs out to continue with their college education. Those who had the financial means moved to other countries. And some, unwilling to compromise on their freedom of religious expression, dropped out from college. I felt so sad for them. Quite frankly, my friends and I didn't know what to do. We all made our decisions individually. I decided to attend classes without a hijab. I was practically living a double life, one in the campus and the other one outside the campus. I was extremely disappointed and distressed.

I did not go to Tajikistan during the summer break of the second year. Instead, I attended a personal development and book-reading program with my dear friends. Together, we prepared meals, engaged in spiritual reflection, and rested our weary souls. We got to know each other more than ever. I realized only years later that those programs had provided me with much-needed nourishment for my mind and my soul.

Hizmet[27]

I was now a whole different Farzona than a few years ago, thanks to Zulal who, years ago, had invited me to a gathering in a masjid for the first time on a Kandil[28] night, all the time that I had spent at her family's house in Izmir, then meeting Semra and her friends in Edirne, and finally the two years that I had spent in Istanbul where I visited so many religious and historical places and helped so many international students like me. I'd now learned that all the things I had been a part of were associated with the "Hizmet Movement." At this point, Hizmet had become an essential part of my life. I think I can describe Hizmet as cultivating relationships based on honesty, pure intentions, and living in harmony with people from every faith. Hizmet is like finding the priceless treasure that you had lost some time ago. Once you found it, you should protect it dearly.

---

27 Hizmet is a transnational civil society initiative that advocates for the ideals of human rights, equal opportunity, democracy, non-violence, and the emphatic acceptance of religious and cultural diversity. This widespread movement began in Turkey as a grassroots community in the 1970s in the context of social challenges being faced at the time: violent conflicts among ideologically and politically driven youth, desperate economic conditions, and decades of a state-imposed ideology of discrimination that mandated a particular lifestyle.

Over the years, Hizmet has transformed from a grassroots community in Turkey to a much wider global effort with participants from all walks of life. Their work is centered upon promoting philanthropy and community service, investing in education to cultivate virtuous individuals, organizing intercultural and interfaith dialogue events to promote peaceful coexistence.

Hizmet participants are inspired by the ideas and example of Fethullah Gulen, a Muslim scholar who has expressed the belief that serving fellow humans is as serving God.

For more information about Hizmet, please see www.afsv.org

28 See footnote 14 on page 24.

For me, Hizmet was first Zulal. She was pretty much the living, breathing embodiment of Hizmet. She could have stayed in her own room at her parents' house and live very comfortably. Instead, she had chosen to stay in the dormitory to share a small room with other five girls, just to be close to the students like me and to take care of them. That was Hizmet. It was a way of life, it was unselfishness and self-devotion. For me Hizmet was being Zulal. If she had not looked after me during those days, I wonder what kind of a person would I have been?

Back to **Tajikistan**

In 2001, I graduated from the Yildiz Teknik University with honors and only in two years, by overloading my class schedule and even taking classes in the summer breaks. During those two years, I also had the opportunity to take care of many students from Central Asia, just like me. We had come together many times, and cooked Tajik and other Asian cuisine food. We had stayed away from alcohol and parties where boys and girls were mixing together. I had finally found a community where I truly belonged. They weren't just my friends, they were my family. After graduation, we had several talks about what to do next. Surely, the conditions in Turkey were not perfect, but all those places and people I loved in Turkey were sufficient for me to stay. Yet, after giving serious thoughts, I decided that going back to Tajikistan made more sense.

So, right after I received my diploma, I returned to Tajikistan. I was now a graduate of a top Turkish university and well-versed in Turkish and English. Numerous Turkish companies had started operating in Tajikistan; finding a job at any one of them wouldn't have been too difficult, at all. I, on the other hand, had a different career planning in my mind. I knew that Hizmet movement had many schools in Tajikistan and that they provided a very high-quality education. I just wanted to work in one of those schools. I knew that I couldn't be hired as a teacher but still applied to the school in Dushanbe. When they told me that they had an opening for a secretary, I said happily: "Sure, I'll do anything!" My mom and stepfather were one more time stunned by my decision. Everyone around me had so high expectations from me, but I didn't care and began working as a secretary in the Hizmet school.

Cihat

Only one month after I started working at that school, the mathematics teacher surprised me with a marriage proposal. His name was Cihat. Apparently, he was working as a teacher in that school for the last three years. He had graduated from one of the top colleges in Turkey and then came immediately to Tajikistan. Almost all the teachers in the school were affiliated with Hizmet movement. In total self-devotion and sacrifice, they had accepted very low salaries: 50 USD in a month for singles, and 100 USD for married teachers. Again I didn't mind that these salaries were so low. I had a couple of meetings with Cihat during which we have talked about general things and tried to get to know each other better. To tell the truth, marriage was not a thing in my mind, but somehow a voice in my head was telling me that he was the right person. Hence, I accepted his proposal, without hesitation.

Cihat came to our house to meet my mom and stepfather. Recently, my mom used to tell me that she didn't want me to marry someone from Turkey so she was not eager to meet him at all. However, after she met Cihat, she had changed her mind because he was really a very respectful man, he had a classy presence, a brilliant education, and a successful career. My stepfather told me that it was totally up to me. And my mom said that she would give us her blessing only on one condition, that we should organize a great wedding ceremony!

The thing is, Cihat's budget was clearly not cut out to fund the kind of wedding my mom had wanted, and it would be even very difficult for his family to come from Turkey all the way to Tajikistan for the wedding. As a matter of fact, in the last three years, he was able to save only 600 USD, that was it. What could be done with that kind of money anyhow? As things usually went with friends in Hizmet, all the teachers, administrative personnel and their families mobilized to help us as much as they could. Cihat was staying in an uptown house together with some other single teachers. They told him that they would move out so that we could live there after the wedding. The house was furnished, so we didn't have to pay any money for furniture or other items. The rooms were small, and the living room was kind of ragged. But who cared really? We didn't even have a proper bed, we had put two sofas together to make a bed. The floorboards creaked and groaned at the slightest provocation; the squeaks and scratches of mice greeted us from beneath, every now and then. The house was quite unfit for a bride, but this was the best we could have. My mom was so disappointed and even angry, but after a while she came to terms with it all and helped us quite a bit to improve the house.

Our wedding ceremony was held in a large hall as my mother wanted and around 350 guests attended. Some were teachers from neighboring cities, even from neighboring countries. At my mom's request, alcohol was served in one part of the hall. It looked like nobody was uncomfortable with this arrangement. The administration of our school had paid so much attention to the ceremony. Even a singer was hired who sang popular songs all night long. An announcer from a local TV station was making the announcements. All the money that Cihat had saved for the last three years was pretty much gone that night, but my mom was quite happy.

Well, there was no honeymoon. Two days after the wedding, Cihat and I returned to our jobs. Soon, I had different responsibilities at school. Because of my fluency in English and aptitude in mathematics, I was now frequently attending classes as a substitute teacher. On top of that, I was also working to counsel the alumni who recently had graduated from our school. And there were class trips organized to Turkey and I had a role in those trips, too. So, every day was quite full of different activities. During the summer breaks, I was attending the summer camps with the students and taking care of them as a teacher and a big sister. My students had become a vital part of my life.

When my first child was born, another layer of responsibilities was added to my very active life. But my passion for education had not diminished through time. In fact, it had only grown stronger. In 2005, I enrolled in a local university to get a degree in "Teaching English." That program was four years long and I completed it in three years. In the year of graduation, I had my second child. I was now officially an English teacher.

In 2006, Cihat became an administrator at the Hizmet school in the city of Tursunzoda, Tajikistan. The intensity of our work has increased even more in that school.

Almost **Dead**

I still haven't forgotten the exact day. It was a Monday evening, the 17th of February 2008. I had just finished up another exhausting day at work and arrived home with my two children; one 3 years old, and the other 18 months old. I was also five months pregnant with my third child. My house chores were the same as ever: sit one of the kids on the sofa in the living room and go into the kitchen with the other one to put some water to boil on the stove. That is what I did that day, too. My younger child began playing with the toys on the sofa. I was in the kitchen with my 3-year-old one, who was drinking water from his cup. In order to prepare dinner, I filled a pot with water and put it on the stove. When I rubbed the match head against the red strip on the side of the matchbox, an ear-splitting explosion went off. It was such a loud explosion that the nine-floor apartment building shook as if an earthquake happened. I felt a sharp pain in my hand. My ears were not hearing anything after the explosion. I vaguely remember the kitchen door lying on the floor and all the windows smashed. Shattered glass was everywhere on the kitchen floor. When I felt pain in my face, I walked towards the bathroom instinctively. But then I saw our apartment's front door which had flown off its hinges. I remembered my children and raced back to where they were. My sensation was so impaired that it was as if I wasn't feeling anything at all. The darkness of the evening had turned into a bright and pure white light, which I couldn't explain how. I could hear my neighbors in the floors above and below, in total chaos. People flew down the stairs three, five steps at a time in their desperation to escape the building. When I rushed to the living room, I cried "Children!" There was no answer. "Mehlikaaa!" I screamed. No answer again. I rushed to the kitchen. The table had flipped over. The glasses and plates lay on the floor, broken into pieces. "Mehlikaaaa! Nagehaaaan!" I hollered again. I went back to the living room, which wasn't any better of a sight. The rug had somehow stuck itself firmly to the ceiling while the window AC unit was dismantled and lying on the floor. Surprisingly, the bronze plates on the wall were stayingexactly where they were. The words Allah[29] and Muhammad[30] were written on these plates. Seeing those plates intact gave me some hope and comfort.

I couldn't find Mehlika and Nagehan anywhere. I was crying their names nonstop and turning over every bit of furniture in panic to find them. Again vaguely I remember that out of nowhere, a man grabbed me by my arm, took me out of the building, and put me into a car. Everything was happening so fast and I could hardly react to anything with my impaired sensation. Then I saw her, my three-year old daughter, next to me in the car. Pointing to my hand she said: "Mommy, what happened to your hand?" The last thing I remember before I lost consciousness was a feeling of relief.

I don't know who had brought me and my two children to the hospital. Glass shards had embedded themselves in my younger daughter's head. They took her into surgery and removed around twenty of them. My hands had suffered slight burns. My dress was completely burned but there was no burn damage on my body. The eyeglasses that I was wearing had somehow protected my eyes and eyebrows but the heat had fused part of my glasses' frame with the back of my ear.

---

29 Allah is the name of the God Almighty in the Arabic language. Allah is the personal name of God. The word Allah is never used for any other being or thing. Islam advocates the belief in the absolute unity of God. Allah is recognized through his attributes and there are over 99 such attributes mentioned in The Holy Quran, the book of Muslims. For example, Allah is Most Gracious, Most Merciful, Lord of All the Worlds, Master of the Day of Judgment, The Provider, The Sustainer, Most Gracious, Most Loving. These attributes are invoked in prayers and also every Muslim is encouraged to adopt attributes of Allah in the journey of life.

30 Prophet Muhammad (Peace be upon Him) (570 Mecca – 632 Medina) was divinely inspired to preach and confirm the monotheistic teachings of Adam, Abraham, Moses, Jesus, and other Prophets (Peace be upon Them all). He is believed to be the Seal of the Prophets within Islam, with the Quran as well as His teachings and practices forming the basis of Islamic religious belief.

While all these were happening, Cihat was at school, busy with unloading a new delivery of school supplies. He came to the hospital as soon as he got the news. By the way, I never criticized him for spending so much time at work. I was not different than him, anyhow.

The news of the explosion reached my family members very fast. During that chaos, my young aunt was told that my two children and I died in the explosion. She was pregnant at that time and upon hearing that, she had a miscarriage. Oh my dear aunt! She was like a second mother to me. In the coming years she had other children, but she never forgot that first child whom she had lost in her womb.

They had not told my mom and stepfather about the explosion at first, they told them that I was admitted to the hospital because I was not feeling well due to pregnancy. But when they arrived the hospital and witnessed all that chaos, they realized that something else was happening. When my mom entered into my room and saw my burned face, she fainted.

So how did that explosion happen? That day in the morning we had left the fire burning on the gas stovetop to keep the house warm. That is what we used to do in the cold winter days. I had also lit the gas stove in the living room and left it on. While we were all at school, at some point during the day, the municipal gas supply had been cut off. With nobody at home to shut the stove off, once the gas supply had been restored, it began to flow freely into the house and accumulated until I arrived. In my haste to prepare dinner, I had not noticed any gas odor and had lit a match.

The doctors in the hospital told us that actually my condition was not good and I had to be transferred immediately to another hospital in Dushanbe, where there was a special burn center. Wrapped in a blanket, they put me on a stretcher in an ambulance. The road conditions were not good, they were quite damaged. Hence it was quite a bumpy ride.

They didn't give me any painkillers because I was pregnant. I was writhing in pain. At the burn center in Dushanbe, doctors from the birth center, ear specialists, and burn specialists examined me one by one. They were especially surprised to see that my eardrum was not ruptured.

What about the children? There was not even a scratch on my 3-year-old daughter who was in the kitchen with me. My 18-month-old daughter who was in the living room at the time of the explosion had a brain trauma and had to stay in bed for two weeks. My mom and my friends helped us so much during that time period so we recovered in a short amount of time.

Well, you might ask how come I had not smelled any gas when I entered the apartment. The thing is, natural gas has no odor. Usually, gas companies add a harmless chemical to give it a distinctive smell, like heavy rotten egg or garlic. Apparently, to decrease the cost of operation, the gas distribution company hadn't added that chemical into the pipeline. As a result, several gas explosions happened that year in the city. Many apartments were collapsed and people were heavily injured. We had heard that in some incident a big piece of glass was launched across the street through the open window, into the heart of an old man while he was sleeping.

Only three weeks after the accident I could see my children again. My swollen face, bruised and darkened lips, and missing hair shocked them so much that for a long time they didn't want to come near me. Some of my friends suggested that I should receive additional treatment in Turkey. One more time, we went to the country that I loved so much, this time wounded. The doctors and other personnel had taken such good care of me in that hospital, which was founded and run by Hizmet movement at that time and seized[31] by the government after the coup

---

31 Since 2016, Turkish authorities have dismissed or suspended more than 150,000

conspiracy in 2016. We didn't stay too long in Turkey and returned back to Tajikistan. Our students were waiting for us in the school.

As I had mentioned above, the bronze plates on the wall with the names of "Allah" and "Muhammad" had stayed intact during the explosion, without any damage whatsoever. Eventually, this became a story that people were telling each other. One of my friends said to me: "Farzona, you were always telling us how important performing the salat is and how it would protect us. Now I see it clearly!" In the morning of the day of the explosion, we had a meeting at school. I had suggested to read the names of the Ashab-i Badr[32] during the meeting for the sake of blessing. It was not something we used to do, I just had felt like it. Later in the day, I had talked to another friend about salat and how important it was in our lives. That day we had prayed a lot. I think it was due to our prayers that our lives were saved that day. Thank God!

And then something unimaginable happened. My mom said that we were probably saved because of our prayers. And soon after, she began to pray five times a day. I had learned about salat from my beautiful sisters in Turkey, and now my mom, thousands of kilometers away, was praying next to me. I couldn't be happier. I will keep my sisters in Hizmet always in my thoughts and prayers.

---

civil servants and government workers, including more than 60,000 police and military personnel and more than 4,000 judges and prosecutors, arrested or imprisoned more than 100,000 citizens, and closed more than 1,500 nongovernmental organizations on terrorism-related grounds, primarily for alleged ties to the Hizmet movement. An estimated $35 billion in businesses and business assets, including from media outlets, schools, universities, hospitals, banks, private companies, and other holdings were confiscated since 2016 by the Turkish government.

32 Ashab-i Badr is the general name given to the 313 companions of Prophet Muhammad (Peace Be Upon Him) who participated in the Battle of Badr, which took place in 624 around Medina between the Muslims of Medina and the Mecca's ruling Quraysh army. This first battle marked a turning point for the early Muslim community from a defensive stance toward one of stability and expansion.

Brazil

Years were passing by. In 2009, my husband Cihat received an offer from a Hizmet school in Brazil to work as an administrator. We accepted the offer immediately; neither I nor Cihat had any questions, doubts, or expectations as we were flying there. We didn't know how much we would be paid, we didn't know anything about the climate, people, or the culture. We didn't ask. It was sufficient to know that we were to continue in Hizmet. If anything, we were really excited that we would serve in another country, literally on the other side of the world. Here I was, leaving my home country, just like thousands of Turkish teachers had left their country to serve in all continents of the world. It took around 40 hours to arrive in Brazil which was around 9,000 miles away from Tajikistan. The language, religion, culture, food…everything was so different. We couldn't find a proper place to live in at the beginning. The single teachers at the Hizmet school were sharing an apartment. They emptied that place and we moved in there. Adding to the list of the rocky start was Cihat's mandatory military service. Right after we moved in, he left for Turkey for two months.

I was now alone in this new country with my three children, 4 years old, 2 years old, and a newborn. In the mornings I was dropping my children to the daycare center and then taking Portuguese lessons from a private tutor for two hours. I focused on two things during that early time period: Settling in and learning Portuguese. The cost of living in Brazil was much higher than it was in Tajikistan. We had a limited budget. I attended the Portuguese class only for two months, at the end of which I was speaking and writing this new language. You might wonder how I was able to learn a new language in only two months. Well, I motivated myself constantly. I spent long nights reading and writing in Portuguese. I copied the passages in my exercise books line by line, down to the last letter. Each transcription bestowed new words upon my expanding vocabulary; I tried to use each word I learned while shopping around the day after. I was trying to write my own sentences every day, around a page, and then showing it to my tutor who was revising and correcting them. Listening and reading obviously help while learning a new language, but it is writing which carries you far away.

It wouldn't be an exaggeration to say that the constant studying gave me severe headaches; I even developed writer's calluses on my fingers. At the end of those two months of extreme hard work, I had lost approximately 25 pounds.

Meanwhile, I have made Brazilian friends and invited them to our house for lunch or dinner. Shared meals and cups of coffee opened ample room to learn about Brazilian people. Some friends from Turkey who had been in Brazil for more than five years and who still couldn't speak Portuguese were quite baffled. I was now speaking in seven languages: Tajik, Uzbek, Russian, Turkish, English, Persian, and Portuguese. Well, soon I would add Kurdish to this list when we would move from Brazil to yet another country: Iraq.

After completing his mandatory military service in Turkey, Cihat came back and started to work in the Hizmet school where the education language was English. Passionate as ever, he wanted to increase his experience in teaching and administrative work, but his health soon started to deteriorate. He was suffering from diabetes and high blood pressure which was caused by the humid climate of the city that we were living in. Diabetes had also caused some damage to his nerves, his feet were going numb at times. It would be more appropriate if we were to be employed somewhere else. So, after one and a half years, we were assigned to a Hizmet school in Iraq.

Iraq

We came to Iraq in March 2010. For the second time in less than two years, we had to adapt to a new language, culture, and lifestyle. We'd picked Iraq because of its relative proximity to Turkey where Cihat could have a better healthcare. Additionally, the dry climate in Iraq was good for his health problems. The quality of the homes was really low, electricity and water often went out, but we adapted. It's actually quite strange how sometimes the challenges in a place can make you love that place even more.

I started teaching in the Hizmet schools and had the opportunity to teach and guide hundreds of students. I made many new friends and received countless favors from them. I hosted many trips to Turkey for students and their parents like I did in Tajikistan. I cannot forget those trips, they were simply amazing. Meanwhile, I also had the opportunity to get to know Cihat's family in Turkey more closely.

The year 2013 was one of the toughest years for me and my family. My husband Cihat was appointed as a consultant for a school to be opened soon in China. I was left alone in Iraq with three children. Managing schoolwork, housework, shopping outside, and taking care of three children by myself was incredibly overwhelming. All I could do was pray, trust in Allah, work hard and never give up. Cihat eventually returned one year later but his health had deteriorated significantly. The diabetes had led to severe wounds in his feet; doctors were even thinking of amputation. Thank God, only a small part of one of his feet was cut off in a surgery and he didn't lose his foot entirely.

While dealing with all sorts of difficulties in life, I had never stopped my journey in academics, and in 2016 I received my Ph.D. degree in "English Education Sciences."

We have been living in Iraq since 2010. Since there are so many things to talk about, it will be better to leave it for another writing, maybe.

Behnan

I think my brother Behnan got lost between the lines, so let me say a few words about him. During his years in high school and then in college, I have tried to support him. After he had graduated from a Hizmet school in Tajikistan, he came to Turkey and attended Istanbul Technical University. During his third year, in 2016, he was arrested in the wake of the July 15 coup conspiracy, like tens of thousands of other people. Apparently, his crime (!) was having stayed in the houses belonging to Hizmet movement! Believe it or not, staying in the Hizmet houses, and reading certain books and newspapers were sufficient for one to be arrested during those years. The Turkish Embassy had sent a letter to my poor mother in Tajikistan stating: "Since your son Behnan has participated in terrorist activities in Turkey, he has been arrested by the Turkish law enforcement authorities." Many Central Asian students like Behnan would receive their dues from arrests made on similar grounds, and some of them were eventually deported.

Behnan stayed in prison for four months. He told me later how he had so many difficulties to find a place to live after he got out of the prison. There was so much chaos and turmoil around him that he is still trying to complete his degree in his fifth year of college. He had always been a hardworking and brilliant student. I am regularly sending money to my brother so that he can get his college degree. There aren't enough words to express the discontent I have over what happened to my brother or the way the Turkish government handled the so-called-coup and the aftermath of it. The decency that we have had in our lifetimes makes us show respect to those people who are in the government. I wouldn't use any inappropriate words against them. But let me say at least this: My brother has never hurt anyone in his life, and never behaved disrespectfully against his mother, father, teachers, friends, and neighbors. It is such a shame that a beautiful person like him was labelled as a terrorist!

Persecution

Behnan couldn't leave Turkey, but thousands of people began to leave Turkey following the events of July 15th. One of the women I had met here in Iraq had a particularly moving story of her own. Her husband had died from cancer while working in Azerbaijan. She had moved to Turkey with her three children, but in 2016, she had migrated to Iraq after learning a warrant had been issued for her arrest. She couldn't bring her children with her. She was living upright by herself and had never lost her perseverance and determination. Having a master's degree in psychology, she could analyze in depth what people have lived through and what they have felt under the oppression. After a while, we couldn't help but ask ourselves: "What's keeping us from helping those who couldn't escape from Turkey? What can we do for them?"

Words led to actions. We interviewed an audience of men, women, and their children—about twenty in total, who had escaped from Turkey. We asked them several global-scale questions and analyzed their answers. The results were surprising, even for us. Because of the traumatic events they were exposed to, the immediate result related to the children was capiophobia, the fear of the police. Some symptoms included anxiety, shaking, loss of control, and excessive sweating. Actually, this fear was visible in adults as well. Another result of our study was due to the extreme financial problems they had since they had left pretty much their everything while escaping from Turkey. They were suffering from the financial trauma with emotional, cognitive, relational, and physical symptoms triggered by significant stressors such as poverty, homelessness, food insecurity, and unemployment. These could have a lasting impact on one's mental and physical health.

Actually, some couldn't overcome their trauma. A woman who'd spent only one night in jail in Turkey threw up for days afterwards. Totally unwilling to eat, she lost weight to the point of emaciation. It was not uncommon to torture the inmates psychologically and physically in Turkish prisons.

Another result was that those who were arrested and stayed in prison for some time were suffering from flashbacks which is quite common in PTSD (post-traumatic stress disorder). They struggled to cope with flashbacks and dissociation, which occurred mostly as a result of encountering triggers that remind them of the traumatic event they experienced. These people that I met had not even sworn in their lives, not even any light swear words. While under arrest, they were exposed to extreme insults and abuses. It is a fact that psychological stress is associated with greater risk for depression, heart disease and infectious diseases, among many other severe health problems. We didn't have a chance to study this further in detail.

One of the individuals we interviewed could not even complete the interview because while answering our questions, she grew paler and paler until she fainted on the spot. They were under extreme stress and anxiety.

I couldn't come to my senses for days when I listened to an event that took place in Turkey. Whenever I think of it, it still cuts me to the heart. The parents of a five-year-old were imprisoned.

The authorities didn't give the child to the grandparents although the parents wanted them to. Instead, the child was put into an orphanage. After many days of struggle and legal battling, the grandparents brought the child to their home. For weeks the child refused to talk and when he finally talked, he said: "They beat me so much there calling me the son of a terrorist (!)"

While conducting our research, our goal was to let the rest of the world know about all these cruel events. So we applied to present the results of our research at a conference in Europe. It wasn't easy to get a visa but eventually we were accepted. If I were the citizen of another country or if I were to live in a more developed country, I would do everything to give talks at every opportunity. I would explain the Hizmet movement to them. That would be the least I could do to repay my brothers and sisters in Hizmet. These people helped me and millions of people like me all over the world for many years. Their only goal was to help us, to make us better people, to make us know and appreciate our own values and share them with the rest of the world in peace and harmony. They had not only shed light on our lives in this world, but they also enlightened our Hereafter. Now that they are in trouble, it was my turn to help them…and I would do that, I would help them…by any means necessary.

It wasn't like the cracks were invisible before that awful day of July 15th in 2016. Actually one year earlier, in 2015, the Tajik government took over the Hizmet schools, under the influence of numerous demands for their closure by the Turkish government. In one of his speeches, the former president of Turkey had praised those schools: *We regard the Tajik-Turk schools which operated for the past twenty years and the students who attend these schools as an assurance of the friendly Turk-Tajik relations.* What has changed since that speech so that the next president of Turkey took every step to shut down Hizmet schools not only in Tajikistan but also in every other country in the world? And while all these were happening, that former president did not even utter one single word of support. Instead he conveniently stood silent and supported the oppression. For shame!

Due to the ongoing persecution in Turkey, we have not been able to go there since a long time ago. We are especially concerned about the possibility of Cihat getting arrested and imprisoned in Turkey since he has worked in many Hizmet schools.

I am writing all these in July 2019. As of today, Nagehan is sixteen, Mehlika is fourteen, and Aslı is eleven years old. For three years they've been unable to visit their homeland. Nagehan wanted to attend medical school in Turkey. She has been an excellent student in high school; however, her path to any college in Turkey is blocked by Turkey's Ministry of National Education, which doesn't recognize diplomas earned at the high school that she has been attending. Her school has international accreditation and offers a strong, rich curriculum, but it doesn't matter to the Turkish government, they just labeled it as a school with terror links! What a shame!

It has been three years that my children cannot see their close relatives and this affects their psychology quite a lot. I am just trying to do my best, under these circumstances, to motivate them. Nagehan had scored 1250 on the SAT test as a sophomore. Hopefully she can get better scores in her senior year and carry herself through the doors of the most prestigious colleges in the world.

Gratitude

Recently, I have been hearing many complaints about Hizmet movement, mostly from outside but some from inside the movement, too. They might be right about some of their criticism, after all we need to be open to hearing all ideas, even the ones with which we disagree. From my personal standpoint, I can say that I have learned so much from the people in Hizmet. I had not known anything related to my religion until I had met them. Only after meeting my sisters in Hizmet I found God, and my life got a purpose and meaning. Many people of Hizmet have died since the coup conspiracy in 2016. To criticize Hizmet would mean to ignore and negate all the wonderful deeds of those deceased. Much of the criticism is callously destructive; insulting, even. Whereas Turkish people can receive religious education to some extent, at least learn about its basics through different means, people like me who were born and raised in some other countries often couldn't. We don't have the same resources in our home countries. I knew almost nothing of religion or faith. How terrifying would it be to live for a lifetime without knowing God and then die upon that state! Even my husband or my daughters cannot understand this because they were raised by religious people. I had no one around to teach me about God. My sisters in Hizmet saved me. They prayed for me, they cried for me, they shared their time, their money, their everything with me. My opinion is that, despite everything, we shouldn't talk against the general character and stance of the Hizmet. There is a big difference between constructive criticism and blatant insult.

Just imagine how many people Hizmet saved from abandoning their faith. It takes so much serious work to carry other people's burden and to lift them up. If we see anything wrong, we should be doing our best to correct it, in patience and with respect. Badmouthing only divides us, makes us weak. We must love each other and move as one. May Allah bless us all with success, health, happiness, patience, and strength. May Allah be forever content with the brothers and sisters in Hizmet. Those who have died, may Allah bless their souls and grant them the highest place in Heaven.

Every day I deeply thank Allah for His uncountable bounties. I am so grateful for the Hizmet, for all my friends in it, for all the amazing work being done in the world. Thank you for being so unselfish and devoted! Thank you for not forgetting Nigeria, Tanzania, Tajikistan, and Mauritania… thank you for being everywhere! What kind of life would I have or would millions of people everywhere in the world have, if you had not come to our countries? You could as well stay in Turkey, have a regular job, and live comfortably. But you didn't do that. You have left your comfort zone and have performed an act of heroism. And now, after all the oppression since the July 15th coup conspiracy, although the people of Hizmet have suffered so much in the hands of the cruel regime, none of them has any regret about their past actions. Yes, not one single person in Hizmet has any regret whatsoever! The difficulties just increase their perseverance and dedication. Their determination to achieve universal peace only increases.

Zulal was the first person I had known in Hizmet, almost 30 years ago. Since then I have known so many people. Other than some small personal mistakes here and there, I can say without hesitation that I have never witnessed any wrongdoing, neither have I sensed any malice. They have lived honest and selfless lives.

The thing is, maybe all this suffering in the recent years is for us to increase our motivation. Maybe we are literally forced to increase our efforts to build on this momentum and achieve an even better future for the entire world. Maybe the hardships of today will whip us and our children into action so we may continue to pursue even bigger charitable acts.

Additionally, it seems to me that our children who attend school abroad have wider horizons than those staying in their home countries. They know that they need to learn different languages to travel around the world. They know how to adapt and integrate into different cultures without losing their core values. They become aware of the wider world and have a true sense of their own role as a world citizen.

Memories

As I've mentioned above, I've never met a person of bad character in Hizmet. I can't remember someone ever breaking my heart. In life, you don't get along with everyone around you. But every single person I have met in Hizmet was caring and responsible.

Years ago, in 2000, while I was a college student in Istanbul, I had written a poem about my dear friends in Hizmet, with the title "Crowd of Angels." I was living in the district of Besiktas at that time, taking classes in the summer school. They were indeed like angels: When I got sick, they rushed and took care of me…if I needed something, they provided it to me. On my birthday, they were together with me with many gifts. With their limited budget, they used to buy all sorts of pastries from that bakery in Besiktas, just to make me happy. How could I forget these people? They were as nice to me as my own mom, if not nicer.

A few days before my graduation from college, while I was walking with a friend, I saw a beautiful pair of shoes. It was a bit expensive for my budget. Two days later, my friend brought me a gift bag with a box in it…and yes, it was that pair of shoes inside the box. How can I forget that dear friend of mine? She was a student like me, on a limited budget. I can give you many other similar examples. I learned from them how to eat only a few bites and offer your guests abundantly when the food was not sufficient for everyone, how to take care of your friend when she was sick, how to help your friend while moving into another house on a rainy day and at the end of an exhausting day to leave with a genuine smile and lots of prayers, how to feel the heartache of someone so far away as if your own heart aches, how to help other people selflessly just for the sake of the content of Allah, and how to live a life full of devotion and with minds and hearts so focused to unconditional love and compassion. A huge shame would be on me if I were to criticize the beautiful people of Hizmet!

While we were living together in an apartment that didn't have a laundry machine, my housemate used to bring my laundry to one of her friend's apartments to wash them there, air dry them on the balcony, fold and bring them back to my room. In Istanbul, I had lived in a dormitory for one year. One night, when I was studying very hard, one of my friends visited me with a grilled cheese sandwich saying: "You are studying a lot, you need to eat a bit." So many wonderful memories, impossible to forget!

And of course, Zulal, my dear Zulal! After I got married and had children, she invited us to her house. She was a medical doctor then. She had prepared gifts for all my family members. She even gave us many extra gift bags and said: "Please give these to whomever you want to." My mother-in-law was with us at that visit. Zulal had paid so much attention to her especially after learning that she had cancer. Later, she used to call my mother-in-law on a regular basis.

No one in Hizmet expected anything in return from me, no one ever asked anything from me, either. Their only motivation was the content and pleasure of Allah.

The more I talk about those good times, the more I remember.

One day, walking to school with a friend, I had told her how much I loved halwa[33] dessert. That same afternoon, she had already made that dessert and left it at my apartment before even I got back home. I was just speechless! Whether it was Izmir, Edirne, or Istanbul... wherever I was, I found the same love and compassion from my dear sisters in Hizmet.

Wearing hijab in colleges was a problem in Turkey in 1999. Hizmet affiliated schools and dormitories were under enormous pressure from the government. Since some of the dormitories and student houses were shut down, including the one I was staying in, I found myself temporarily staying in the apartment of a sister who was married. That night I heard her husband yelling and her crying. In the morning, I even saw bruises on her face. She apologized and said: "My husband was a bit drunk last night; sorry for disturbing you." Apparently, her husband was against Hizmet and had strongly disapproved of his wife hosting someone from Hizmet, unfortunately, in a quite violent way. Well, how strange life is!

Let me tell you this: getting divorce in Tajikistan is extremely easy. You don't have to look too far to see children who live either with their father or mother alone. In my marriage, I had some small problems, too, every now and then. But my husband, being a man of Hizmet, never drank, smoked, or engaged in other vices. In the end, I even owe my happy and peaceful marriage to Hizmet.

On August 14th, 1999 I went to Tajikistan. Three days later, on August 17th, a catastrophic 7.6 earthquake struck Izmit and the neighboring cities in Turkey, including Istanbul. My birthday was on August 20. So many of my friends called me that day from Izmit and Istanbul to celebrate my birthday, when only a few days ago their

---

33 Halwa is a sweet which is made of wheat flour, sesame, or semolina and combined with honey or sugar. Other flavorings, such as nuts, dried fruits, or chocolate are often added.

houses were totally collapsed by the earthquake. It has been 20 years since then, and we still talk to each other frequently and visit each other when we have a chance.

Afterword

So many things have changed since I had met Hizmet decades ago, especially after the coup conspiracy in 2016. I tried to do my best to find ways to help my dear sisters in Turkey. One of them told me: "Farzona, it never occurred to me that one day we would be in such deep trouble, and you would support and help us." How could I leave them alone during those difficult times? I only wish I could do more to help.

In 2019, I was talking on the phone with another friend who had been in prison for some time after 2016. She is actually a journalist and author. Now they live in a farm. The first thing she told me on the phone was: "Farzona, do you need anything? Can I help you with something? Please tell me!" I pray that more people follow her example of altruism.

These people were my role models. They have always approached me with patience to smooth my sharp edges, to transform me into someone better. They were not intimidated by my thorns and prickles, they never gave up and never left me behind.

People associated with Hizmet who are still in Turkey go through extreme difficulties, while the ones who have left Turkey cannot return to their homeland anymore to see their parents and other family members. My daughter wants to go to Hacettepe Medical School in Turkey. The chances are slim to none, but I believe God will open other doors in the future.

While I was attending the college in Istanbul, I used to read books whenever I was on a bus. During one of those bus rides, I had finished the book "Eternal Light", written by Fethullah Gulen[34]. It was a book about the life and teachings of Prophet Muhammad (Peace Be Upon Him). I remember that moment: I looked at the sea, then closed my eyes and got immersed in thoughts: "Thank God, I have known you O Muhammad, the Dear Messenger of God!" All my friends have a deep love and respect for Him. We Muslims follow Him, He is our guidance. Every day, He is in our thoughts and prayers.

Fethullah Gulen has written many books about Rasulullah[35] and reading those books we learned about Him and we loved Him. In Turkey, since 2016, it is sufficient enough to be labeled as a terrorist if you keep a book of Fethullah Gulen. They throw you in jail for several years because of this crime.(!) A few days ago, my mother called me from Tajikistan and told me that so much defamation has been going on in the media against Hizmet and asked me what to do with the books of Fethullah Gulen at home. Hundreds of thousands of copies of his books were burned in Turkey. I said: "It is up to you, mom." She replied: "There is no way I can burn them or trash them. On every page, God and His Messenger are mentioned."

We make mistakes; we're human, after all. We can't tear down a

---

34 Fethullah Gulen is an Islamic scholar, preacher and social advocate, whose decades-long commitment to education, altruistic community service, and interfaith harmony has inspired millions in Turkey and around the world. Described as one of the world's most important Muslim figures, Gulen has reinterpreted aspects of Islamic tradition to meet the needs of contemporary Muslims. He has dedicated his life to interfaith and intercultural dialogue, community service and providing access to quality education. For more information, please visit www.afsv.org

35 Rasulullah is an Arabic term that translates to "Messenger of Allah" which is used to refer to Prophet Muhammad and also every other Prophet, such as Adam, Noah, David, Abraham, Moses, Jesus, and many others (Peace Be Upon Them All). Messengers are believed to have been sent by God to different communities during different times in history. They all preached the same core beliefs, the Oneness of God, worshipping of that one God, avoidance of idolatry and sin, and the belief in the Day of Resurrection and life after death.

movement for a few wrong actions of a few individuals. I love Hizmet with all my heart. I am 40 years old and the mother of three children, but there have been many times that I prayed for the God to take years from my life and add them to the life of Fethullah Gulen. Every day I pray for his health and well-being. It was through him and his books that I learned about Rasulullah and my religion.

There are so many things I want to do but I don't have the means. People like me need Hizmet. My children need the people in Hizmet. None of us is immune from going astray, regardless of how young or old we are. We have to be on guard constantly if we want to protect our heart, our soul, and our faith. And for that, we need good people around us. We need to be in a constant relationship with Allah and His Messenger. Whenever you show a weakness towards evil, ask yourself the following question: "Would Rasulullah be happy and content with me if He were to see me doing this act?" This is the way that I learned by reading the books of Fethullah Gulen.

I believe in the power of prayer that can transform our lives. One prayer I've repeated over the years is as follows: "O Allah, give me the strength to accomplish tasks that take other people days or years, in seconds." I've repeated this prayer countless times in my life. Prayer provides synergy, so don't hesitate to ask others to pray for you. It doesn't even matter who prays for you. You would never know whose sincere prayer would be accepted by God. Allah has beautiful names and attributes such as Aleem[36], Hakeem[37], and Hafeez[38]. Memorize, recite, and embrace them. In order to be successful in this life and the Hereafter, focus and work hard, stay away from people, places, and habits that would mislead you, and pray: "O Allah, give me success. Enable me to surpass my limits." There are some special times during the day, like the dawn, which begins with the first sight of lightness in the morning and continues until the sunrise. That is also when the muezzins[39] call atop the minarets[40] in the mosques for the first prayer of the day. I wouldn't miss that time and pray in devotion when it was so quiet and peaceful outside. It was not seldom that I could literally feel the peace and serenity surrounding my mind and soul.

Reading, working hard, and praying. In life, we encounter many strange events, twists of fate, or incredible strokes of blessing. All are somehow influenced and fulfilled by our prayers. There are hundreds of thousands of brothers and sisters in Hizmet serving in different countries across the world. Please unite with the people of the countries you live in! Please grow harmony, love, and peace!

---

36 Aleem is one of the attributes of Allah mentioned in the Quran. His knowledge encompasses everything that is visible and is hidden, and that is kept secret or made public. He knows all that is in the heavens and on the earth, as well as the past, the present and the future. Nothing is hidden from Him.

37 Hakeem is one of the attributes of Allah mentioned in the Quran. He is the One Whose wisdom is perfect, free from any error or misunderstanding. His divine will is executed with His divine wisdom, which means He does everything in the most appropriate way in the best place and time.

38 Hafeez is one of the attributes of Allah mentioned in the Quran. He is the All-Preserver, the All-Heedful, the All-Protecting. He is the One Who creates and preserves the worlds and what they contain. He is heedful of all we do and He protects us from things we do not even realize.

39 The muezzin is the person who proclaims the call to the daily prayer (şalat) five times a day at a mosque.

40 See footnote 20 on page 28.

For four years now, I have lived away from Tajikistan and Turkey. I dream and hope that one day I will be able to return and visit one more time the tombs and dargahs of Yahya Efendi[41], Eyup Sultan[42], Hayrettin Tokadi[43], and many others.

I dream and hope…

---

41 See footnote 22 on page 31.

42 The Eyup Sultan Mosque is in Istanbul. The mosque complex includes a mausoleum marking the spot where Abu Ayyub al-Ansari, the companion of the Prophet Muhammad (Peace be upon Him) is said to have been buried. A mosque complex was constructed on the site in 1458 by the Ottoman Sultan Mehmet II only five years after the conquest of Constantinople (Istanbul) in 1453.

43 Hayreddin Tokadi (16th century) is an Ottoman Islamic scholar. His tomb is located in the city of Bolu, at a distance of around 150 miles from Istanbul.

II

IN THE RIGHT PLACE, AT THE RIGHT TIME

as told by
Aram Reman

FOREWORD

Many countries in the Middle East endure ongoing wars and conflicts, Iraq is one of them. The authorities in those countries make decisions on behalf of the people and drag them into unnamed fights and wars. People who have not even once been treated humanely have been let to fight against each other for economic and political ambitions for decades. As a result, the ordinary people live in constant poverty and misery. This is the fate of this geography.

Here children play war games among each other. The childhood of the main character in this book is full of constant fear and longing. He learned words about war at a very young age. Among the people who are of the same land, culture, and nationality but yet who are constantly fighting against each other, he and his family wouldn't have too much choice but constant struggle, immigration, or exile.

But surprisingly a glimmer of hope would be seen in this desperation one day. Actually, the origin of that hope wasn't so far away. A group of teachers coming from a neighbor country, Turkey, would be the guides of thousands of children who have had nothing but pain and sorrow in their lives. These volunteers would do everything they can to teach love, peace, human values, and unselfishness by facing up against all kinds of difficulties with strength and determination. And they wouldn't expect or ask for any payoff in return for their efforts.

Fate of **my Country**

My name is Aram. I learned the meaning of my name years later. It was a common name given to children at the time I was born. I was born in Soran. If you want to know where Soran is, it's a little town in Iraq bordered on one side by Iran and on the other side by Turkey. A sparkling river runs through my beautiful town. In the summer months it is emerald green around, and in the winter we have so much snow. My town is a settlement close to a magnificent canyon, waiting to be discovered at the foot of the imposing Mount Korek, the mountain which means a lot to me and my family. In Iraq, my ill-fated country, there are constant wars, fights, sufferings, and tears. Those wars and domestic conflicts are all about the natural resources and political and economic interests. For decades, brothers have been made enemies to each other, and of course, international deep plans have never been absent in my country. From a very young age, I have witnessed numerous perplexing and disturbing events.

These burning and devastating wars and civil conflicts continue around my town; in Mosul, Ramadi, Kirkuk, and in the neighboring country of Syria, as if they will never end. I feel so sorry that the life of a human, known as the most excellent creature, is so cheap, and can be taken with no reason. The clean-hearted people in my country have also been fighting against deep poverty and misery for so long. I feel disgusted by the ones who cause all of this, but there is not much I can do. Unfortunately, most of the people who are suffering are the young ones who have lots of hopes and dreams about life. Older people say that this is the destiny of this geography, and they helplessly try to endure the ongoing misery…

My Father and
the Years of Exile

When I was born, my father was a soldier, a captain, in the Kurdish military force known as Peshmerga. My father spent part of his life in the Iran-Iraq war, which continued for eight years. He also witnessed many civil wars and conflicts, and later on, he lived in exile. In 1984, because of Saddam Hussein's unbearable oppressions and cruelties, he left the city and joined the opposition groups located in the mountains. You might, of course, have heard about Saddam. For some people, he is the greatest Iraqi hero; for others a cursed tyrant; and for my father, he is the man who forced us to live through "the dirtiest war ever." I remember those time periods, albeit only vaguely.

I was born when my father was in the mountains. Let the word "mountain" not scare you. It didn't scare my father. He was together with hundreds of other people, fighting against the regime forces of Saddam, demanding their fundamental human rights. These weren't big battles, but there was a lot of suffering. Do I need to remind the world that around 5,000 people—mostly women and children--were killed by the regime of Saddam using chemical weapons in the city of Halabja in March 1988?

My father is a man who said farewell to lots of things at an early age: his beloved home, his pregnant wife, cuddling and smelling his soon-to-be-born baby, dinner tables with family and friends, and many other beautiful things you can imagine. In the fight against Saddam, that local group didn't have a chance, and unfortunately, many people were killed. Those who survived were exiled to Dohuk from Soran, together with their family members. When children, women, the elderly, and sick people were stuffed into trucks and taken to exile camps, I was only a child. The poor people who were taken to the camps had just a few clothes with them. My mother still talks about those camp years with sorrow.

We stayed in that camp for more than five years trying to survive the difficult conditions, until one day my father took all the risk and managed to take us out of the camp. We escaped to the city of Sulaymaniyah where we stayed in relatively better conditions. In the mid-1990s, the people in Iraq started to fight against each other. The civil war was never ending. Soon my father had to choose a side and found himself fighting in battles. There was so much pain all over the country. Thousands of people were killed or injured. Many more had to leave their houses and everything they had in life.

As a result of these fights, extremely strict security precautions were implemented at the entrances and exits of all settlements. We had to live in Sulaymaniyah like prisoners; we couldn't go anywhere else. There were not too many safe towns around where we could go, anyhow. Our hometown Soran was only four hours away from Sulaymaniyah, yet it was so risky to take that trip. One day my father had learned that his father passed away in Soran, but he couldn't even attend his funeral, whom he loved so much. I remember how sad and devastated my father was during that time period.

The Eid **Days I Hate**

Eid days have always been very important in our culture. Because we couldn't go anywhere from Sulaymaniyah, I used to spend most of the Eid days alone at home. Early in the morning, my friends and I would gather to play, but after a while most of them would leave to visit their aunts, uncles, and other family members. Then I would go home and just watch television. And during these times when I had to stay at home, I always watched Turkish channels and series like Çocuklar

Duymasın (Children Shouldn't Hear), En Son Babalar Duyar (Fathers Hear Last), Deli Yürek (Crazy Heart), Beyaz Show, and İbrahim Tatlıses Show. And thanks to these television programs, I learned Turkish very well. For me, watching those television shows was like escaping to a friend. I still don't like the Eid days, actually I hate them.

At the beginning of the 2000s, people in my country broke with the past and finally made peace. They said that it was time to come together, and they embraced one another. People who have shared the same culture and faith in this land for a long time witnessed that it wasn't so difficult to live in unity and cooperation once again. My family and I were very happy because we could finally travel freely from one place to another in our own country.

Pain **Never Ends**

It was the beginning of 2003, after 8 long years, when we could finally visit my grandparents and other relatives who were still living. I always remember the excitement of that sweet moment of reunion. How can I forget the happy sound of drums when we arrived in Soran and people welcoming us with joyful folk dance?

It is, of course, not possible to talk about everything that we lived through during those wars, exiles, and anarchy. What my father once said to summarize those years is quite revealing: "There have been many days in my life when loaded guns were pointed at my forehead. I hope I don't hear the sounds of war on the day that I die." For me, especially on each Eid day, I remember those bitter childhood days which are full of sadness, helplessness, and desolation.

Years later, I realized that even the mountain ranges of this country, which have witnessed all kinds of clashes, the stones containing every shade of yellow, the rivers flowing tirelessly, the dusty roads, and the tired streets seem to grudge the peaceful days. That's why you can't have much hope in these lands of constant chaos and you can't have big dreams. For example, if you are a teacher it is very difficult to motivate your students to be successful. You can't just say, "If you study a lot, you will accomplish great things and may even get rich." Because of the serious destructive force of negativity in our country, the eagerness of children and young people to find meaningful lives is lacking. Of course, children cannot live without dreams. Every child growing up in this land has one of two dreams: either being a doctor with a white coat or being a soldier wearing a uniform. The reason is simple: Because of wars and poverty, doctors are very needed here. And unfortunately, military service is a way to make a living.

I was never interested in these occupations. My father had always encouraged me to pursue the career that I really wanted. My mother, who cannot read or write, wanted me to be a doctor. After finishing high school, I studied Petroleum Engineering for two years at a community college, and I found a job at an oil company after graduating. In our country, things to do after finding a job are quite clear: getting married, having children, and raising a family. I didn't have time to think about these. After two years or so, I realized that I was missing something important. Most of my friends who were working in the company could speak English fluently. The oil business required proficiency in a foreign language. So, to advance in this job I needed to learn English quickly. After some research, I found a private university that was good at teaching English. I took the university entrance exam again and enrolled in the Department of English at this university. The main goal of the most students in the department was to become an English teacher after graduation. I was not interested in becoming a teacher. I couldn't visualize myself in the classrooms with 60-70 students, among teachers yelling and even humiliating the poor students. Besides, the salary of a teacher has always been very low around here. So, I didn't want to waste my time and energy on this job. My purpose was just to learn English well.

I enrolled in this university with the financial help of the company I worked for and started studying English. Besides the lessons, we were participating in different activities together with the instructors, both inside and outside of the university campus. We were spending so much time together. And after two months I began to observe that there was an important difference in this university from other places I had studied. There were many people who were helping us in the design and implementation of several projects. We were feeling the sincere attention of our teachers all the time who genuinely cared about any problems we had. Until that year, in any school I had attended, I used to stay away from the teachers. Like most of the other students, I used to do anything to avoid any interaction with the teachers, because they were extremely rigid. If anything, students were afraid of the teachers. At the community college that I had studied in earlier, the instructor-student relationship was also very distant. But this time, in this university, everything was so different. These instructors were ready to sacrifice their everything for the students. We were struck with admiration.

Most of these educators were from Turkey. There they were: Turkish teachers! From elementary school to the high school, we were told and read books about how Turks had persecuted Kurdish people in different time periods in the past. The textbooks were full of these kinds of narrations. Was there any proof for these claims? Who wrote these textbooks and why? I wouldn't know. But I do know that despite all these claims, most students, when they went home from the school, they watched Turkish movies on TV, listened to Turkish songs, and decorated their rooms with the pictures of Turkish artists. I guess they didn't want to believe all those they were told at school. They just wanted to pull thick curtains over the past. When you get in a taxi around here, it is quite likely that you hear popular Turkish songs, and you may even see the pictures of Turkish artists decorating the inside of the taxis.

Turks or Kurds?
We are All Human!

From elementary school to the high school, we were told that Turkish people were very cruel towards Kurds in the past. Well, the grandchildren of those people were now our teachers, and they were the best that we had ever seen, the most caring and compassionate. They were never criticizing anyone's religion and never discriminating between students of different ethnicities, whether Kurdish, Turkmen, or Arab. As academicians, they would listen to the students' troubles with patience and try to find solutions. They would invite their students into their own homes and prepare food, and sometimes they would even travel four to five hours to visit our families bringing gifts. When everybody else was spending their time with their own families on the Eid days, these teachers were visiting their students' families, without expecting anything in return. My family had never seen a teacher in our house, so they were feeling so special and happy during those visits, especially my mother. We would all wear our beautiful traditional clothes and prepare the most popular local dishes for food. In our culture guests are important, but having these teachers as guests was particularly significant for all of us.

There were also students from Turkey in our classroom. We tried to get to know each other closely. We would talk for long hours to each other. We drank tea made in Turkish or Kurdish style and ate stuffed vegetables we brought from home. They offered us the famous Turkish dish Chee Kofta. At the beginning, we approached each other with hesitation and carefully weighed the words in our conversations. But it soon became clear that the only obvious difference between us was this: Turkish people were drinking tea with only a little sugar or no sugar, but we were filling the tea glass almost one-third with sugar and then stirring it for a minute. Turkish people would make stuffed vegetables with just certain vegetables, whereas we would make the same dish with almost any vegetable. They would make Ashura (Noah's pudding) with sugar, we would make it salty. Of course, there were some other small differences between us, but we were the people of the same land, after all. The intentions of the Turkish students and teachers were straightforward and clear. One of our teachers said, "Our aim is to serve human beings wherever they are, without distinguishing their color, race, or belief. For us, there is no more sacred and precious matter other than calling for people to do good."

Our teachers and Turkish friends at the university invited us to Turkey during the summer breaks. We went to Turkey in groups with great excitement. They entertained us in various cities of Turkey as if we were very valuable guests. They provided us with the best accommodations; they cooked for us and offered us their best traditional dishes. In some cities, some of the local businessmen hosted us in their homes. These businessmen, who employ hundreds of people in their workplaces, served us food and tea with their own hands and sent us off with gifts afterward. We were hearing the sounds of azan from the mosques five times a day, and some of our friends were very surprised. We had always been told that Turkey was like any other European country, and Turkish people had a European style of living, far from religion. The Turkish films we used to watch also gave us this impression. But we saw that this wasn't true.

While in Turkey, we used every opportunity to observe Turkish people in their own homes, offices, workshops, streets, and bazaars and we also listened to many different stories from them. Here I want to share an incident that happened, as it was told to us during one of these visits. The incident happened in Izmir and probably the man telling the story was the main character in it. We didn't ask, and he didn't tell, either. One night, when he was usually up for the night prayer, he heard some noise coming from the living room. Without waking up his wife, he took his registered gun from the wardrobe and very slowly walked towards the living room. There he saw a young man, holding a flashlight and looking around for some valuables. After a few seconds, the homeowner turned on the lights. The young man froze up upon seeing the homeowner with a gun in his hand. The businessman, smiling at the young man, said, "Take it easy son! Calm down, I won't hurt you. Just sit down please." He was in his twenties, quite skinny and in poor clothes. The businessman asked him about his family, their financial condition, where he came from, where they lived, and how he ended up entering people's houses. The young man told him that his family had come from another city to Izmir to find work, and they had settled in one of the ghettos. He looked for a job for a long time, but he couldn't find one. So, together with a few friends, he began to break into houses. He was crying while he was telling all this. The businessman thought that this poor young man was good inside. While they were talking, his wife entered the living room. She had already woken up to the noises and heard this conversation. The businessman, without embarrassing the young man, whispered to his wife: "We have a guest, please prepare some breakfast for us." They had breakfast with the young man together. He was very hungry. The businessman and his wife stayed on the table more than usual so the young man could eat as much as he wanted to. And after some time, as the young man was leaving their house, the businessman gave him his business card and some money, 500 Turkish liras. Four or five days later, while he was in his office, his secretary informed him that a young man was insisting on seeing him. He came without an appointment, but the businessman met him with a smiling face. They drank tea and had a chat together.

When the businessman offered him a job, the young man said: "After that night I questioned myself and I realized my wrongdoing. I have five friends who are pretty much in the same situation as I am. Actually, they are waiting outside the factory right now, waiting for me." The businessman invited those young men into his office, and he talked to each of them. He gave a job to all of them that day. In time, those young men rose to good positions in the factory. This kind of real-life stories affected me so much during our visits to Turkey.

The **Refugee Camp**

It was 2014, the end of November. I was still a student in the university. One day, the teacher of a debate class, Mr. Numan, invited me to his office. He was one of the most original persons I had ever known, really one of a kind with his artworks and creative ideas especially related to photography and videography. On that day when I entered his office, he wasn't as calm as usual. He was standing, with a worried look on his face. "Aram," he said, looking out the window and pointing somewhere. "There is a camp near us accommodating thousands of people who escaped from Syria. It is in a very poor condition. We accidentally saw this camp while a few other teachers and I were visiting our students' families close by. We wanted to see the living conditions inside the camp, so we went there. It is indescribable how miserable those people are. I wish everyone could go to that camp to see how those people try to survive in very small containers with their crowded families. The terrible toilets and bathrooms cannot be described… Thousands of people have to live behind wire fences near us, away from their homeland, weary and miserable. I cannot forget the children I saw there wearing no shoes. We must do something for them. Maybe we can find a way to provide them a proper schooling. The local people and the government help with clothing and food.

But there are hundreds of children in that camp who take classes in those containers. Why don't we bring a more proper education to those children? Why don't we give a helping hand to alleviate the loneliness of these people? You are a local, you know this country much better than me. Besides, you can speak Sorani Kurdish, Badani Kurdish, and Arabic languages. Would you like to work with us?" I accepted Mr. Numan's offer without any hesitation and said, "Of course, sir! I'm ready to do my best." I had lived in similar camps during my childhood for four years. How can I forget the coldness of the ground in the winter and its boiling heat in the summer while walking with bare feet during my childhood? How can I erase those memories of shivering from the cold and hugging my mother for some warmth? Mr. Numan was someone who liked to act promptly. "OK, then. Let's do some fieldwork first. Let's go to the camp to find out what they need," he said. Next day early in the morning, we were in the camp.

There was a worse sight in front of us than even what Mr. Numan had described. The weather was so hot. Soil and dust were transforming the heat into a giant burning fire. I could only imagine the temperature of the water inside the small tanks which were placed on the roof of the containers. That was the water used for drinking and washing. We saw people waiting in long lines for toilet and bathroom needs, people aimlessly sitting in front of tents and containers, and so many children running around, under extreme heat and dust.

The director of the camp told us that the population of the camp was more than ten thousand and most of them were children. Nearly two hundred fifty children didn't have their fathers and mothers with them. Hundreds of women were widows and were struggling alone to survive. We had seen many pictures about the camp in the newspapers or on TV before, but seeing the situation with naked eyes and witnessing the deep misery was very different. My mind took me again to those years when I had stayed in a similar camp when I was a child. I remembered that feeling of trying to survive desperately, unsure what the future will bring, with no hope.

We asked the camp directors what we could do for them. They said that there were thousands of children in the camp, but they didn't have enough teachers at all. Teachers usually didn't want to work in these conditions too long, after a while they were leaving. The teacher shortage was so severe that in the entire camp there was only one person to teach English to thousands of children. We learned about the details such as how many classrooms are there, how many teachers in each field, how many they need more, etc. We walked through the entire camp, took photographs, and noted the sorrowful stories of the people we talked to. The camp was only five miles away from the neighborhood where the university was, and thousands of people were literally trying to survive in it. We had to act immediately to help them.

A few days later we made a presentation at the university and then recruited volunteers. Fifteen of our friends said, "We are in, too." Other than organizing a teaching-oriented group, we also formed another group of volunteers to collect clothing and food aid. Within a few days, the entire department was mobilized with excitement. Our intention was pure and sincere, we were genuinely concerned about the situation and we wanted to help in whichever way we could. After a few days during which we took care of some bureaucratic paperwork, we were ready. My appreciation for our teacher Numan had increased even further during this project. It was amazing to witness how a single man's one idea could mobilize so many people so quickly. The sincere actions that someone takes were not to stay unrequited. In general, most people have a feeling for helping needy people, they just need an inspiration and encouragement. In this case, that inspiration was the voice of our teacher Numan.

The was another teacher who had also soon become a very important person and role model in my life. His name was Ibrahim. I learned to finesse the teaching skills from him, inside and outside the classroom. Teacher Ibrahim had shown us many different teaching methods in education related to using technology, giving effective lectures, class control, paying close attention to students, and finding instant solutions for unexpected situations in the classroom. He visited the homes of almost all of my classmates, met their families, and showed genuine care and appreciation to all of us. We were ordinary university students, nothing special. But this teacher showed us that we did matter, we were valuable, we were important.

Thanks to the many different activities we were doing together, like playing soccer or having regular picnics, my friends and I had built strong bonds with each other and with the university. We got to know each other better, listen to each other's troubles, and do our best to help those of us who needed any help. Our university was newly founded and it was growing and transforming steadily. The academic and social activities we were attending were opening up our horizons. I was heavily involved in setting up a radio station for the university, giving presentations at different conferences, joining discussion groups, and having good relationships with my friends and teachers. All of these helped me to grow and transform in many ways.

"We are **Hungry**"

It wouldn't be right if I didn't tell you about Teacher Hasan. He would never get tired of helping others, enjoying his job truly and accepting people as they were without judging. I have learned so much from him. In my view, he is an artist who works very carefully to get a brand-new product from valuable metals or alloys. He created a WhatsApp group for the students staying in the student residences or student homes. The group's name was We Are Hungry, and it was open for every student. When a few students wanted to share something or seek advice for their problems, they would send a message to Teacher Hasan with the phrase "We are hungry!" Our teacher Hasan quickly would gather some food from his house or someplace else, drive to the place where the students were, and would spend some time with them.

Residential life on the campus is boring for most students. This boring and depressing atmosphere only dissipates with different activities. I was staying in a student residence, too. One night a nice food smell was coming from outside nearby. Looking out the window I saw that Teacher Hasan and several students were roasting a sheep on a spit! In a few minutes, all the students in the residence hall were looking out the windows in amazement. There were approximately forty students staying in that residence hall. Teacher Hasan made a hand gesture and invited them all down to join. That night until five am in the morning we were all together. We ate well and plentiful, drank tea, and had conversations about many things. The food was more than enough for forty students, we even took the leftovers up to our rooms. Teacher Hasan used to surprise his students from time to time. One day he had cooked Uzbek Pilaf for all the students in the residence hall. We were enjoying the opportunity to try different types of dishes thanks to him.

The things Teacher Hasan did for us weren't just limited to food. Students who would have a cold or a headache would first visit his office. He had around ten different types of herbal tea boxes in his office. After learning about our health complaint, he would boil some water in an electric kettle and choose one of the herbal tea types in his office. Soon we would be enjoying a nice cup of tea. Of course, it wasn't medicine, but it would make us feel so good psychologically.

I had the experience of drinking those herbal teas five or six times in his office. Each time I felt much better.

In this city, there are small tea houses serving breakfast early in the morning. Teacher Hasan used to take his students on Friday mornings to these tea houses to have a splendid breakfast together, without discriminating between rich or poor. During those breakfasts, we were talking about many different topics and getting to know each other much better. I don't think I can forget these beautiful memories in my lifetime. Perhaps all these stories that I am telling you sound quite simple. But in our country, having a teacher who so much cares about his students is a very big deal.

Our teachers Numan, Ibrahim, Hasan, and many others became our role models and showed us, by living, the ideal teacher profile. We have learned that being a teacher was indeed a very powerful thing, you could change people and eventually the entire society. All of these teachers were living very modest lives, without any expectations. Before Iraq, they had worked in many other countries, voluntarily. They devoted their lives to education. Their self-sacrificing way of giving themselves for others was beyond description. Even our own closest family members wouldn't show this much care and compassion for us. They were living in modest houses like ours, they were struggling with power and water shortages and trying to solve their heating problems using naphtha. Their income was very limited, but still they were spending a significant amount of it for their students. Some of our teachers were able to speak the Kurdish language fluently. Didn't they have their own personal problems? I am sure they had, but they had never mentioned them to anyone. They were spending all their time and energy for their students.

Changing **My Way**

Thanks to these teachers whom I took role models for myself, my perspective on life changed a lot. I didn't care about the oil business anymore. Within the Syrian camp project, I was helping needy students while also learning more and more about the teaching profession each day. It was indeed an amazing feeling to give and expect nothing in return. Witnessing students learn and seeing them happy as a result was my biggest reward. I was getting warmer to the idea that I could choose the profession of teaching after graduation. Like my teachers, I could serve my community and even the entire humanity. I could spread the kindness, goodness, and solidarity around the world. After all, life was not about making more money and getting rich; it was about touching people, entering into their hearts, and helping as many people as possible. Only then we could live peacefully in this world. During my junior year in college, I decided to pursue teaching as a profession.

It was not only me whose views about life have changed during the Syrian camp project. The majority of my friends have also decided to become more involved in education. As a matter of fact, from seventy-five students who had graduated from our department in the university that year, sixty-five of them have found jobs in the education sector. I started to work as a teaching assistant at the same university. My friends and I had decided to do meaningful things in our lives.

It is 2020 now. I am still busy with the organization of teaching in the camps in Mosul and Syria. Through the years, I got more and more attached to the children in the camps. Perhaps this is why I want to keep going with these camp projects as long as possible and not to do anything else. I remember the classroom environments that I have been to earlier in my life where students were not even allowed to drink water when they were thirsty. This was no more the case in our classes. We created classroom environments filled with love, respect, and trust, ensuring that all the needs of the students were addressed.

I would like to tell you about some of my memories related to the camp. At the end of one teaching day, one of our colleagues got on the bus, crying. She was crying because that day several students in her class were wearing no shoes; they had come to class barefoot. Well, this was actually not unusual, many poor students were coming to classes either barefoot or with simple slippers. But what was different this time was that our colleague was wearing on that day a pair of shiny and stylish shoes. She told us: "All the students were looking at my shoes. I was so ashamed of myself. I took them off and continued the lesson barefoot, just like them." The next day, several of us went to the shoe stores nearby and purchased one hundred pairs of shoes. I wish you could have seen how happy the children were when they had received the new shoes. Seeing them so happy made us very happy, too, and increased our motivation and dedication.

We often observed that the students were very tired and weak, especially in the mornings. After searching for the reason, we learned that the children were coming to the early morning classes without having any breakfast because the breakfast was distributed in the camp a bit late. This is when we decided to bring some fruit juice and biscuits to the classroom early in the morning. Meanwhile, we were informing people in the community about our work in the camp and asking if they could offer any help. Through the efforts of a friend, a school director in England contacted a sports club and convinced them to donate sweatsuits, shoes, and different kinds of clothes. It was one of the happiest days in the camp when those clothes had arrived and were distributed to the students. They couldn't believe their eyes, they were showing their new clothes and shoes to each other, holding them in their arms like a mother holding her baby, touching them gently, and dancing around in circles. We danced with them together and joined in their joy. We helped most of them to put on their new clothes and shoes and took so many pictures that day. In retrospect, I now think that although it was a beautiful day, I wish these children had experienced these kinds of joys and celebrations not in a camp, but in their own homeland, in their homes, with all the family members around them. I wish they could live a life like the other children in the world, where simple things like having a new pair of shoes don't turn their day into a festival. I wish that this camp life, which was not too different than an open prison, would come to an end once and for all. It is so unfortunate to see that wars, forced displacements, refugee camps, and the resulting pain and suffering have only become routine around the world.

Although the education facilities in the camp have become better in the last five years with the help of UNICEF, the limited number of video projectors and computers are still not used efficiently because of the frequent power outages. Also, in a country where the temperature reaches 120°F in the summer, air conditioners are seriously needed in the classrooms. Unfortunately, there are not enough air conditioners in the camp, and again the power outage causes problems. The volunteer group of our university aims to provide a generator for the camp school. It is difficult given the circumstances, but not impossible.

Our other goal is to improve the teaching methods of the teachers at the camp. We try to find qualified educators to give seminars about this. I think we can achieve this goal too. The children in the camp also need a library, a social activity center, and sports facilities. Why not?

I want to emphasize it once again. I wish that no children or adults were forced to live in these terrible conditions, and that everybody could live enjoying peace in their own country. I wish politicians would no longer make decisions sitting around a table which results in the clean water of rivers, lakes, and seas becoming dirty and congested. Let people live in peace and let them not be forced to leave their countries, suffer from permanent physical and emotional injuries, and exhaust their lives in miserable conditions.

They Sailed **to Tomorrow...**

My teachers' lives have been severely affected, too, by recent political decisions. Shortly after the coup conspiracy on July 15, 2016 in Turkey, my teachers were held partially responsible for it! They were accused of being terrorists by the Turkish government[44]! Their passports were seized, and they couldn't even obtain official documents for their newborn children. With no assistance whatsoever from the Turkish consulates, they faced many different problems such as not being able to extend their visas when they were expired. There was only one thing they could do: Leave Iraq and try to go to some other countries where less problems were caused by the influence of the Turkish government. Unfortunately, my teachers Numan, Ibrahim, and Hasan had to leave the country like many others. Each of them went to different countries. What is even worse, these amazing education volunteers couldn't continue educational activities in their new places, either. Last I heard, Numan was working two jobs as truck driver and a barber. Ibrahim

---

44 After the coup conspiracy in 2016, more than 160,000 innocent people lost their jobs in both public and private sectors, with accusations and unjust convictions of being connected with the coup attempt. The state of emergency, which was announced on July 20, 2016, gave the Turkish government unchecked powers - in the disguise of combatting terrorism - to persecute thousands of people with no accountability and to undermine the fundamental principles of a democratic society and the most basic principles of universal human rights and values such as freedom of expression and freedom of the press. Today, tens of thousands of highly qualified professionals such as judges, prosecutors, doctors, teachers, journalists, academics, and military officers have been detained and imprisoned in Turkey due to bogus terrorism charges. Around 5,000 of them are women, along with nearly 345 children who stay with their mothers in prisons. Hundreds of thousands of people have little or no hope of surviving the grueling atmosphere in Turkey, and as they are banned from leaving the country, they have no other choice but to flee at the risk of losing their lives by crossing the borders via dangerous routes. Some of them have not survived this difficult journey.

and Hasan have changed many different jobs.

Since they left, the breeze of war blows again in this geography, and quite strongly. The civil war in Syria is still ongoing and the violence is spiraling throughout the entire country. Regional violence and ethnic clashes are on the rise again in Iraq. The global plans and interests of the American government and the political and religious influence of Iran are never ending, as a result of which bombs are exploding in every corner of my country. Soldiers from near and far countries and from different ethnic groups are killing each other and the Iraqi citizens. I am not interested in any politics at all, but I have been more and more confused since some time ago. On the one hand, there were my teachers from Turkey who had devoted themselves to our education and made us love Turks and the Turkish culture; on the other hand, the ongoing wars and military operations…It has become a routine event that every now and then a lot of women and children escape from the war in Syria and come to the refugee camps here, which are already overcrowded. It is just an endless cycle of suffering and struggling to survive.

If my teacher Numan was here, I'm sure he would come up with some new projects. Teacher Ibrahim would emphasize the new methods of efficient teaching, and Teacher Hasan would demonstrate new ways of taking care of students. This land needs them so badly. But they are not here anymore…a piece of us is missing now. But I know they will come again one day and show us that the remedy for suffering and poverty is just educating people and living altruistically for others. They will be a fresh breath for the education of our children. Recently, I listened to the poem of Adnan Yucel, a Turkish poet, and thought of my teachers with a deep longing in my heart:

"Love" said all the gurus of life
To appreciate the beauty with passion
And to fight for the sake of that beauty

…
Violets pop upon us one day,
Lilacs start smiling.
What will leave behind from these days are…
Those who sail to tomorrow,
And those who fight for tomorrow.

I'm going to repeat myself again, but I must say it. I believe that showy lessons, fancy presentations, and papers with many citations are not the heart of the matter when it comes to education. The teacher should first get to know, understand, and conquer the hearts of the students. And to do that, teachers should spend time with students doing different social and cultural activities. A teacher isn't someone who just lectures in the classroom and then goes home. As a matter of fact, teachers should look for opportunities to help educate anyone and anywhere, not only their own students and not only in school. I try to follow the footsteps of my teachers. I might not be as passionate as they have been, but I am doing my best to take them as my role models. I have big dreams.

My name is Aram. I learned the meaning of my name only later.

It means "Peace".

Note: *I have recently completed my graduate studies and received a master's degree in the Department of Teaching English. I'm happy to work full-time as an instructor in the same department where, years ago, I had enrolled with the intention of only learning English. Those oil companies still offer much higher salaries, but I am not interested. My biggest goal is to produce teachers for my country and for the entire world. Teachers who are passionate, kind, and selfless. Teachers like Numan, Ibrahim, and Hasan.*

III

HOPE BEYOND THE BORDER

as told by
Turkmen Hanim

They **Came**

I tossed and turned in bed, restlessly. Flickering my eyes open, I glanced at the clock on my phone: It was 3:55 AM. With effort, I rose. Clutching my stomach, I tiptoed to the kitchen, fetched a glass of water, and returned to bed. I drank the water in a few gulps. For five months, I had abstained from painkillers and would continue to do so. I began reciting the Ikhlas[45], one of the chapters I read most often in the Quran. It brought a measure of relief. All the while, I anticipated a message on my phone, a simple phrase: "I bought simit[46]." Perhaps this message would ease my agony, if only slightly. I turned off the light and lay down slowly, letting the words of the İhlas escape my lips into the silence of the dark room. Sleep was an elusive dream.

It was 4:35 AM. I jolted awake at the sound of the doorbell ringing three times quickly. Could it be my husband, really returning with simit? He had planned everything meticulously, assuring that nothing would go wrong. It seemed some mishap had occurred, forcing him to return from wherever he had been. Yet, he made it clear during our last farewell: he wouldn't come back home, no matter what. He had pondered over this tough decision for days: to stay or leave. He had chosen to leave.

A sudden cramp seized my stomach. I took deep breaths. The doorbell rang again. Reluctantly, I decided to answer it. Holding my stomach, I shuffled towards the door, my mind swirling with

---

45 A chapter in Quran which displays the attributes of God that help us give an idea of how we should think about God: "Say: He is God, the One and Only; God, the Eternal, Absolute; He begetteth not, nor is He begotten; And there is none like unto Him."

46 Simit is a ring-shaped baked product made with wheat flour and encrusted with of sesame seeds.

possibilities. Maybe it was my sister; it had been a long time since her last visit. The likelihood of my in-laws coming was next to none. I wished it were either of them. My husband's parting words echoed in my mind, "They will definitely come to the house. Don't open the door immediately, stay calm, don't panic! Act as if I am with you and pray! Stall them as much as you can," he had advised.

I peered quickly through the peephole of the door. The long-awaited had arrived, just as my husband had warned. To steady my trembling limbs, I continued taking deep breaths. The visitors outside rang the doorbell again. I waited in silence for a moment, trying to decide what to say.

It had barely been a minute when they started pounding on the door's knocker. A stern male voice demanded, "We know you're in there. Open the door!" I tried to calm myself. Gathering my wits, I responded loud enough for them to hear, "My husband is not home. I cannot open the door." For a fleeting second, I feared they had come for me and braced myself to hear them say, "We don't need your husband." But they didn't.

Looking through the peephole again, I saw them conversing. On just two of them, vests clearly marked "POLICE" were visible. The other four were indistinguishable in their disheveled appearance. One had a face so darkened it seemed almost black. The same voice then threatened, "Open the door! Don't force us to use our methods. Or we'll enter as we see fit." I was at a loss for words.

"Officer, my husband is not here, I can't open the door. I don't know when he'll return."

"Then contact your husband immediately. He needs to come here. Don't keep us waiting too long!"

Peering once more through the peephole, I saw only two men

remaining. The others had likely gone to their vehicles. Despite trying to remain calm, anxiety was building with each passing moment. The men were resolute; they would enter by any means. I thought of messaging my husband to alert him but then refrained, fearing the message might be intercepted by the police. Even if I sent it, he might not see it; his phone could be off.

Before deciding whether to open the door, I hurriedly scanned the house, something my husband and I had repeatedly done before. Just in case, I glanced at the spines of our books, double-checking for any titles or authors that could cause suspicion.

I looked out the living room window. A police patrol car was outside. Two officers were lighting cigarettes, laughing, and chatting. They seemed worry-free. For the sake of the baby in my womb, I tried not to let my worries and suspicions grow further. About half an hour later, the doorbell rang again. Until that moment, I had been trying to maintain control, but the sound of the bell startled me. My heart raced, my hands trembled.

The voice of the police had echoed through the apartment building, demanding and loud.

"Ma'am, did your husband call? When is he coming?"

"I don't know. He hasn't called."

Another officer, with a sterner tone, insisted,

"Call him. Otherwise…"

Otherwise, they would forcibly enter. Several of my husband's friends and two of mine had already been arrested. I knew our turn had come. More than my own safety, I was worried about the health of my baby.

The message I had been waiting for from my husband still hadn't arrived. His phone seemed to be off. Clearly, he hadn't reached his destination yet. I had to keep the police at bay as long as possible. If they interrogated me, I prayed to God for the strength to not let anything slip.

Years **Ago**

Years ago, my brother and sister had studied at schools opened by Turkish education volunteers. My parents had enrolled them in those schools because they provided quality education. I didn't get the chance to study in those schools, but years later I found myself in a beautiful city: Konya. You know, the city which is famous for Mevlana[47], Alaeddin Hill, Karatay Museum, Selimiye Mosque, famous flatbread with meat, oven kebab, and many other beauties... I spent four wonderful years there. I stayed in a student dormitory for one year, and in student houses for three years. I made unforgettable friendships, and I had friends whom I considered siblings. I had the opportunity to visit many cities during the holidays, and I was also a guest in my friends' hometowns. I walked the streets of Fethiye, which smelled of pine trees, ate delicious food in Gaziantep, and met leblebi[48] in Çorum... I tasted different flavors everywhere I went, and I also told the hosts about the delicacies and beauties of Turkmenistan at every table. The aesthetics of the motifs on our carpets, the elegance of our Akhal Teke horses, the importance of the old caravan roads, the hustle and bustle of our weddings... Sometimes I compared the Turkmen culture with

---

47 Mevlana Jalaladdin Rumi is a 13th century Muslim saint and Anatolian mystic known throughout the world for his exquisite poems and words of wisdom, which have been translated into many languages.

48 Leblebi is a snack made from roasted chickpeas, sometimes seasoned with salt, hot spices, dried cloves, or candy coated.

the Anatolian Turkish culture. We shared many folk lyrics together, lyrics written to praise our similar yet different cultures.

After four years, Turkey had become like my own hometown. My family in Turkmenistan was eagerly awaiting me as soon as I graduated. I thought a lot about going back to Turkmenistan. I could find a teaching position at the schools where my siblings graduated, but the schools had been closed with various made-up excuses a year before I graduated from college. The closure of schools that had been educating very successful students for many years occurred due to constant pressure from the Turkish government and its president.

After graduation, I decided to go to another country, perhaps somewhere in Europe or America. However, while I was in contact with people who would help me with this, I received an acceptance from the Marmara University Department of Computer Education, which I had previously applied to for graduate school. So, I postponed the idea of leaving Turkey for a while.

Leaving Konya was bittersweet, yet the prospect of moving to İstanbul filled me with excitement. Thankfully, I had no difficulty finding a place to stay; I started living with people like me who were in graduate school or teaching. My goal was to be an academician at a university, eventually.

I met **Him**

I devoted myself entirely to my graduate studies. I was very busy. As in Konya, I sometimes went to the hometowns of the four friends with whom I shared the same house. One of my friends, whose family lived in one of the nearby cities, was inviting us to her house on holidays. I met her brother at a dinner. He was very polite, a gentleman who gave people confidence with his eyes, and was listened to in the environments he spoke. We talked about the schools we were attending and our goals throughout the dinner. The rest developed on its own. You know the classic story: A man and a woman see each other and then take a path to love. Our situation was also similar, more or less. In those days, I was like the state of the lyrics of the song by Bulutsuzluk Özlemi:

I've broken the chains,
Set sail to the seas.
Bubbles all around,
Full sail,
As I'm drawn towards you.

Everything is new,
Everything is beautiful,
Everything is different, exciting.
Have I ever been like this?
I don't know if I'm ready.

It seems I was ready, as I said yes to his marriage proposal. Of course, I didn't say yes immediately. Even though my family was far away, they spoke several times over the phone with my prospective husband and his family. In fact, the formal proposal was done through a video call. My father had only one condition: to also have a wedding in Turkmenistan. And so we did. My sister and brother were able to attend the wedding in Turkey. My parents couldn't come because they couldn't get their passports in time, which really upset me, but I didn't reflect it to anyone. I even ignored those at the wedding who treated me like a foreign bride, and turned a deaf ear to their comments:

"Ah, the bride isn't local."

"She has no relatives here."

"She doesn't even know how to make our local dishes."

Does gossip ever end? Yet, I knew some traditional Turkish dishes. Even though I might not know how to make baklava[49] or yuvarlama[50], I had learned how to make dolma (stuffed vegetable dish), and of course, menemen[51]. Since my student years, I had been able to cook all kinds of potato dishes. I didn't pay much attention to the details others got hung up on. My husband didn't have high expectations of me anyway.

I Couldn't **Say**

It was just a few months before I was to start my academic career when the police came to our door. By that time, over a hundred thousand people had been dismissed from their jobs or thrown in jail. In a time when so many were being imprisoned, and thousands had fled the country through either regular means or with the help of smugglers, it was quite ordinary for the police to appear at our door. If I tell you that this and similar incidents began on that ominous night of July 15, 2016, you will understand why the police were

---

49 Baklava is a layered dessert made of filo pastry sheets, filled with chopped nuts, and sweetened with syrup or honey.

50 Yuvarlama is a Turkish soup made with spiced meatballs, chickpeas, yogurt broth, olive oil, and other optional ingredients.

51 Menemen is a popular traditional Turkish dish that includes eggs, tomato, green peppers, and spices cooked in olive oil.

standing at our doorstep[52].

Some saw it as a treacherous plan by a particular group, others as the government's project to eliminate people affiliated with or feeling allegiance to a group. I didn't dwell much on these. I knew the people of Hizmet for their honesty, hard work, sacrifice, and the importance they placed on moral values. Of course, there could have been one or two individuals with bad intentions among them, but I never encountered any. I never thought those people would betray their nation, not at all.

The police were waiting in vain for my husband. Nearly three hours had passed. They knocked on the door again. Looking through the peephole, I saw that one of them was a woman this time.

"Madam, please open the door. We need to search the house."

Hearing the voice of the female police officer somewhat relieved me. After all, we didn't have the kind of books, pictures, or whatever they were looking for. I opened the door. They kindly removed their shoes outside. As soon as they entered, they showed the search warrant and stormed into the rooms. They repeatedly checked the balcony, the bathroom, under the bed, the wardrobes, and inside the kitchenware. Then, they sat in the living room and bombarded me with questions one after another.

"Where is your husband?"

---

52 Since the coup plot in 2016, Turkish authorities have dismissed or suspended more than 150,000 civil servants and government workers, including more than 60,000 police and military personnel and more than 4,000 judges and prosecutors, arrested or imprisoned more than 100,000 citizens, and closed more than 1,500 nongovernmental organizations on terrorism-related grounds, primarily for alleged ties to the Hizmet movement. An estimated $35 billion in businesses and business assets, including from media outlets, schools, universities, hospitals, banks, private companies, and other holdings were confiscated since 2016 by the Turkish government.

"When did you see him last?"

"Why hasn't he come until now?"

"If you are pregnant, then why is your husband not with you?"

I couldn't tell them my husband went to the border intending to leave the country, how hard our farewell was, what we went through while making that decision, and to whom he entrusted me. I could only say, "He had some business to attend to. He is together with one of his friends." After the search and interrogation, they said, "Either your husband comes and surrenders at the police station, or we will come back," and left.

My pain had intensified. I didn't want to alarm my husband's family, so I chose not to inform them about the situation. I tried to comfort myself a little since my sister from Turkmenistan was coming soon to help me. As soon as the police left, a few neighbors came over, and as if the distress I had just experienced wasn't enough, I had to deal with their questions.

"Why did the police come?"

"Why did they wait so long?"

"Really, we haven't seen your husband for a few days either; what's the matter?"

The accusation that hurt me the most was,

"Are you one of those people too?"

What's the matter, neighbors? My husband left, leaving me in this state, with my belly and all. Should he have stayed and been dragged to jail like his friends? Should he have been tortured? And no, we are not those (!) people. My husband is just a man working very hard to serve his country...

Thank God, my sister arrived while the neighbors were still there, putting an end to the interrogation. The conversation drifted to other topics, and they dispersed one by one. After the neighbors left, a few tears fell on my sister's shoulder involuntarily. I had promised myself not to cry my heart out. I recounted everything to my sister in detail. My husband being fired, not finding a job afterwards, the changing attitudes of the neighbors, and most importantly, the arrest of his colleagues one by one, and finally, how we converted the last of our money into dollars to give to human smugglers and his plan to go to Europe via Greece... I told her everything.

My sister said, "You should have gone too... Right, how could you with your pregnancy?" I replied, "For now, there's no arrest warrant for me. Maybe we'll go to Turkmenistan after the birth." My sister smiled bitterly, "The situation is messy there, too. You know they closed the Hizmet schools. They occasionally interrogate those who have studied in Turkey. It's better if you don't come," she said, and I sighed deeply. "Let's wait for news from my husband. God is gracious," I said.

Just a year before, in February 2017, we had traveled to Turkmenistan for our wedding. Immersed in our traditions, my husband, despite not even smoking, was offered alcohol by my relatives, playfully drawn into regional folkloric dances, and even coaxed to try kumis[53]. It wasn't a lavish ceremony, but our traditions were proudly on display. We donned our customary attire, and the bride's and groom's cars were adorned separately. To bless our future with purity and prosperity, white flour was sprinkled on clothes laid over the cars, candies and desserts were distributed, and rice pilaf cooked in large cauldrons was served to all.

---

53 Traditional Kumis is a fermented mare's milk, which has a slightly sour taste.

Embarking on this new chapter in our lives with the love and support of our loved ones, we were confident that our mutual respect and affection would guide us through any challenge. We vowed to always be there for each other, sharing laughter, tears, and a path forward together. Our wedding festivities spanned three joyful days, but an everlasting love had blossomed within our hearts.

We returned to Turkey a week later. At passport control in Istanbul's airport, an unsettling feeling of being watched persisted. When my husband's hand trembled slightly, I instinctively grasped it for reassurance. Thankfully, the process was swift, with no delays or questions. Yet, despite the outward normalcy, a lingering unease remained within us.

The first month of our marriage would bring news of my pregnancy. How could I have foreseen that I would soon regret the pregnancy, unaware of the even greater hardships that lay ahead? My troubles began in the second month of my pregnancy. Due to the risk of miscarriage, I spent most of my days lying down. My husband was finding temporary jobs here and there, but it wasn't comfortable for him. There was no investigation against us after July 15th, but we were on edge. After all, we were both part of the group known as the Hizmet Movement. My husband hadn't stayed in student houses or dormitories due to his profession, but somehow he had been connected to these places. Even if he had stayed, what would it have mattered? Was he going to engage in clandestine activities and betray his country and people?

When five of his colleagues at work were arrested and thrown into jail, he began to feel constantly under pressure. He was either going to be arrested like his colleagues or, like two of his close friends, he would have to flee abroad. We had traveled abroad with our current passports for our wedding, but he still didn't want to take any risks. Probably there was something else and he wasn't sharing what he knew with me. He didn't want to upset me. "It's my turn coming; I can feel it. The noose is tightening," he would say, "Leaving you behind like this doesn't sit well with me."

To which I replied, "I'll manage on my own. It's more comforting for me to know you're safe somewhere else rather than being imprisoned here."

The **Second Raid**

The next day, the doorbell rang insistently. I shuddered. The police were at the door again, but this time it was a different team and they were more numerous. I didn't keep them waiting this time; I let them in. They would have entered anyway! I hadn't received any message from my husband yet, but I assumed he had probably crossed the border by now. Having my sister with me was comforting. They spread out through the rooms, tossing around our beds, clothes, and books. The police from the first search had been replaced by rougher types. Not content with rifling through our books, down to the pages, they repeatedly checked behind, on top of, and underneath the cupboards. They had turned our home into a battleground. At one point, gathering my courage, I asked,

"What are you looking for? Let me help you."

The police officer, with his hair and beard all tangled, retorted,

"Are we supposed to ask you what we're looking for?"

"Well, you know best," I replied, to which he gave me a sharp look and said,

"Of course, we do."

When they couldn't find anything, they started questioning me again.

"Where is your husband?"

"He said he was going to a friend's."

Another officer asked,

"Who is this friend?"

"He didn't say."

"When did he leave?"

"The day before yesterday."

"Why is his phone off?"

"I don't know."

"If you don't know, who will?"

"He doesn't tell me everything."

"Where is his passport?"

"He carries it with him."

"Where are your dollars?"

"We don't have any dollars."

"…."

They asked my sister the same kind of questions,

"Why did you come?"

"To visit my sister."

"Where did you learn Turkish?"

"From Turkish schools."

"Are you one of those people, too?"

"I don't know "those" people," she said, and then they started speaking to her in a mocking tone,

"Should we take you too? What do you say?" It was as if I was facing the police of another nation. My sister turned pale and couldn't answer.

An hour passed. While the inspector leading the raid was questioning me, his phone rang. He answered immediately.

"… Really? Hmm, so he's been caught. Good … very good… Then we're heading back."

He turned to me, almost mockingly,

"Congratulations, your dear husband has been caught at the border."

Congratulations to me!

What kind of congratulations?

My husband was arrested; was I supposed to be happy about that?

What was I supposed to do now?

Who should I inform?

I couldn't tell my own family. My mind was in turmoil.

Then, I remembered the verse in the Quran:

"Be patient, indeed, Allah is with those who are patient."

...and this hadith[54]: "There is something amazing about the believer: all his affairs are good, and this is true for no one except a believer. If good times come his way, he is thankful, and that is good for him. And if hardship befalls him, he is patient, and that is good for him."

I also remembered a phrase that Turks often repeat: "May Allah protect us from worse."

I snapped back to reality when the inspector called out,

"You will find out where your husband is soon enough. I recommend you hire a lawyer as soon as possible."

He turned to his team:

"Let's gather up and leave. We've gotten rid of another one."

One of the police officers lingered behind. He was the last to leave. Making sure everyone had left, he said,

"Find a lawyer immediately. But make sure that you be careful, too."

Who could this well-intentioned police officer be? Perhaps someone who knew my husband. Or maybe someone who couldn't stomach what was happening. But whatever it was, the sincere advice and sympathetic look from one among many officers somewhat alleviated the worries inside me.

After the police left, with the help of a friend, I found a lawyer. He said he would get on it right away. Of course, hiring a lawyer would have its costs. My husband had given most of the money he had set aside to human smugglers for the border crossing. What was left was a bit of money and the gold received at our wedding.

---

54 Hadith is an Arabic word referring to what most Muslims and the mainstream schools of Islamic thought believe to be a record of the words, actions, and the silent approval of the Islamic Prophet Muhammad (Peace be Upon Him) as transmitted through chains of narrators.

It had been over a year since those damned July 15 events had taken place, and my husband had been arrested.

The pains began to surge. I lay down on the bed.

Half an hour had passed when the doorbell rang again.

It seemed the sound of the bell would now become my nightmare. I forced myself up.

At the door, again, were neighbors. They were disturbed by the constant coming and going of the police. They didn't want such things. They asked where my husband was... I underwent another interrogation. I had to endure.

Two days later, the lawyer finally managed to contact my husband. He had only been able to trace him, nothing more.

I was somewhat following the events through television news. Arrests were ongoing in the entire country. My sister also had a general idea of what was happening in Turkey. I explained the details she didn't know as best as I could.

Three weeks after my husband's arrest, the lawyer said that my husband was put in jail and nobody but the lawyer was allowed to visit him[55]. The only thing that the lawyer knew about him was that he was in good condition. That was all. I immediately called my mother-in-law. Initially, I hesitated to tell her. I had a good guess of how they would react, and I wasn't wrong. My mother-in-law, in an indifferent tone, said, "If he was arrested, he must have done something wrong." Nothing had ever struck me as cold and merciless as those words.

---

55 Under the state of emergency the Turkish security agencies had the right to detain individuals in police custody for terrorism or coup-related offences for up to 30 days – a huge increase on the standard four-day period – and they were denied access to a lawyer for the first five days in police custody.

When I shared my situation with a friend from my graduate studies, she mentioned that the upper floor of her house was vacant and told me not to worry about the rent. Without much deliberation, we decided to move. Thankfully, with the help of her siblings, we relocated. I couldn't help but think that our neighbors, who treated us like terrorists under the influence of the media, must have been happy after we moved.

My lawyer informed me that my husband's indictment had not yet been prepared, but he could visit him every fifteen days. However, I was not allowed to visit. Despite my anger, I swallowed it. My husband had believed that the truth would eventually emerge, asserting that a great trap was set for the country. Yet, I wasn't in a state to ponder the internal or external schemes playing out in Turkey. There was only a month left until my delivery. I didn't want to distress my baby any further.

Let me clarify that I too had interacted with the Hizmet Movement, stayed in their dormitories, and met dozens of people. I never witnessed a single word or action that could be deemed as treason against the nation. Their sole concern was education; they talked about investing in people and were limitless in their social services. They established associations and foundations, not only serving in Turkey but all around the world. They spoke of moral values, justice, and putting people first... This is how I saw and understood them. Otherwise, claims of infiltrating the state, lack of transparency, and close contacts with political figures, etc., were beyond me. These were very educated people. What were they supposed to do? Retreat to the villages and become shepherds?

Finally, I received some good news I could be thankful for. My lawyer said that I too could visit my husband every fifteen days. As the visitation day approached, my excitement grew. The sleepless nights lying in bed, unable to take my eyes off the clock, feeling as if I was about to do the most wonderful thing in the world! Only those who have experienced this excitement and anticipation would understand. I hardly slept the night before the visitation day.

Meeting Behind the Glass
and the Stateless Baby

Our conversation took place through a glass window, over the phone, and lasted fifteen minutes. Contrary to what the lawyer had said, he didn't look well at all. He had lost weight and struggled to speak. The first three minutes were spent in tears. Despite my efforts to hold back, I too let my tears flow freely after a point. My tears were filled with longing, anger, and stress... I'm sure his emotions were even more profound. My husband apologized numerous times for leaving me alone. He briefly explained that things hadn't gone as planned and somehow he had been caught. He spoke vaguely. The fifteen minutes ended too quickly anyway.

In the final week of my pregnancy, I couldn't visit my husband. I didn't have the strength. I had intended to, but on the day I was supposed to visit, I started having contractions and we headed to the hospital instead.

And I gave birth. My sister and mother-in-law were with me during the delivery. How I wished I could share my pre-birth excitement, my fears during the birth, and my post-delivery joy with my husband! I longed for him to be by my side as I held our baby in my arms. Well, it was just not meant to be.

Once I had somewhat recovered, my sister and I went to the civil registration office to get an ID for the baby. Unfortunately, they wouldn't issue one. The reason: I was apparently not a Turkish citizen.

Though I was officially married, holding a Turkish Republic marriage certificate in my hand, they said my husband needed to be present for the procedures. When I mentioned that my husband was "inside," the officer said, "We don't know the inside or the outside. Your husband needs to come to us to start the process." The officer could have done it if he wanted to, but for some reason, he chose not to. How long could I manage with just a birth report? How was I supposed to take my baby to the doctor? He was unregistered, practically stateless.

My baby was fifteen days old. His father had not seen him yet. A new problem was on the horizon: my residence permit in Turkey was about to expire. I would need to renew it in a few months. And my fear materialized. They said they couldn't extend my stay because my master's program had ended. Yet, a friend in the same situation had her residency extended. There was something off about this, but I couldn't figure it out. I went to the United Nations representative and explained my situation. They said there wasn't much they could do and that it would be best for me to return to my country. Easier said than done. After the pressures exerted by the Turkish government before and after July 15, 2016, the Hizmet schools in Turkmenistan had been closed, and some members of the Hizmet Movement had been arrested. How could I return to my country?

I knew that soon I would face financial difficulties, as well. I asked my sister to stay with us a bit longer. There were so many uncertainties ahead and I didn't know how to deal with them. But that day was quite important: My husband and our baby would see each other for the first time.

The meeting was again behind the glass. My husband looked incredibly happy. His eyes were shining with joy. He looked at his son's face for minutes, without talking. A few times, he extended his arms to hug him, but he just touched the glass window. I didn't say anything about the ID problem and other difficulties. It was not the right time. The baby was sleeping in my arms.

The day after the visit, a school friend from Konya called me. I could sense the panic in her voice. Many of our friends had started to get arrested, including Kyrgyz, Turkmen, and Uzbek friends who had stayed in dormitories or homes. She warned me to be careful and hinted that my name might have been added to some lists as well. I felt the weight of an invisible oppression. I didn't tell my sister about it. All night long, I tried to find my way through a tangled labyrinth in my mind. What should I do? What steps should I take?

The next day, I went to the lawyer's office. Before I could explain my situation, he mentioned that I could have an open visit with my husband. I was relieved. However, when I shared my concerns, the lawyer revealed more,

"Your friend is right. For over a year now, they haven't spared anyone. Being with a baby or being sick doesn't matter to them. If your name has come up somewhere, that's it. It looks like they could detain you as well. The state of emergency laws are still in effect. People are being detained for even subscribing to a newspaper[56], and you've stayed in their homes. I'm sure you've participated in various activities. In short, it's enough for one of those detained to mention your name," he said.

"What should I do? What can I do with my newborn baby?" I asked. The lawyer replied,

---

56 Tens of thousands of individuals were trialed in "July 15 related" courts, most of them were found guilty and sentenced for imprisonment, for the acts which did not constitute a criminal offense under the law in force at the time it was committed, or even at the time of those trials. Some of those so-called "criminal offenses" were being subscribed to the best-selling newspaper in Turkey, Zaman, which was in circulation since 1986; having an account in Bank Asya, which was one of the biggest banks in Turkey since 1996; and choosing the schools affiliated with Hizmet Movement for your children to attend. Inviting your friends to your house or visiting them in their houses on a regular basis was also considered a crime.

"You could consider taking the risk of returning to your homeland."

"I can't go back, no. I know what awaits me there. It's too chaotic there, too."

"Then you either take the risk and stay here, or..."

"Or what?"

"Or you'll try the same path your husband did. You'll have to finish what he couldn't. Crossing the Maritza River these days doesn't seem too problematic. I'd say go for it. Of course, as a lawyer, advising this goes against the law. But we are living in a time when laws are not being applied. When there's no other option... Soon, there's your husband's trial. He's likely to be sentenced to six years and three months in prison." It was the first time the lawyer had spoken so openly and hopelessly.

While the lawyer's words echoed in my brain, I also envisioned crossing the Maritza River[57]. How could I embark on this risky journey with my baby? I had been following on social media that even pregnant women were being arrested and thrown into jail. It seemed likely that the day I would be handcuffed was approaching. As I was leaving, the lawyer added,

"If you want, discuss it with your husband during the open visit. But be very careful when you talk!"

---

57 Because of the enormous pressures, climate of fear and witch-hunt of Erdogan regime after the coup plot in July 2016, many people have been seeking for the ways to escape from Turkey to their freedom at any cost. One of the ways is crossing the Maritza River at the border between Turkey and Greece. According to the Stockholm Center for Freedom, thousands of people have fled Turkey through the River of Maritza and other means. Unfortunately, many people drowned and died along with their children while crossing the river.

The Final **Visit**

I went to the prison with my baby, filled with the excitement of facing my husband without the glass window in between us, for the first time after four months. It would be the first time he would hold our baby and look into his innocent face. As soon as he saw us in the visitation hall, he rushed over. Without saying a word to me, he took the baby into his arms. For a while, he just stood there, unsure of how to hug, kiss, or talk to him. His tears began to fall on the baby's swaddle. Our baby, opening his eyes to the world with innocence, was looking at his father for the first time. My husband took his tiny hands into his, smelled him over and over, and then kissed him repeatedly. This pure and touching silent meeting between father and child was witnessed by the walls of the prison visitation hall, the chairs, and the tables.

Minutes flew by quickly. Our eyes locked. As if he had just noticed me, he said, "Welcome," and we embraced. I needed to say what I had to say quickly. The word "My dear" fell from my lips and echoed between the walls. That word was like the first note of a song that hadn't been sung for a long time. "My dear, the lawyer bluntly said I should complete the job that you started. Otherwise, I might end up in a similar place as you."

My husband hugged our son tighter. In a sorrowful tone, he said,

"Does that mean I won't see you again?" My voice trembled as I replied,

"How can you say that? Of course, you will see us. You will always be with us," I said, trying to fit all the hope and love in my heart into those words.

"If you need to go, then go. I'll follow you later," he said, giving his consent.

A week after our visit, we were in the courtroom. Every shade of brown I disliked dominated the walls, tables, and chairs. It smelled of ruthlessness and tension. I don't know if such a smell exists, but it had to be a scent unique to that courtroom. I saw my husband in the waiting area before the trial began. The soldiers didn't allow us to exchange even a single word. The trial was very short. The judge didn't even listen to the defense of my husband. There were none of those fervent defense scenes you see in TV dramas. The lawyer was right. My husband was sentenced to six years and three months in prison. The judge pronounced his decision, "Based on concrete evidence indicating a strong suspicion of guilt, the defendant is sentenced to six years and three months in prison..."

Another sentence followed, "Due to the suspicion that the defendant might flee, hide, or has shown signs of fleeing, he is sentenced to three months in solitary confinement..."

Nonsense!

Of the dozen crimes listed, which one had this man really committed?

And other accusations that lingered in my mind:

Attending a meeting on a certain date,

Calling someone from a payphone,

Inciting hatred and hostility among the public,

Attempting to stage a military coup (!)

My baby in my arms, I listened to all the charges, with my mouth agape. None of them were tangible. They were all baseless. His eyes persistently said he didn't deserve any of this.

As my husband, handcuffed, was escorted past me by the

gendarmes, we exchanged glances. Though he wanted to touch our baby, the gendarmes didn't allow it. He boarded the prison van, bearing the weight of a harsh verdict that affected not only him but us as well. No one from his family had come to the trial. They were still angry with my husband and also afraid.

During our last visit, my husband had mentioned the name of a furniture dealer, Mesut. We were supposed to leave the country with the help of him. I went to Mesut's furniture store in the darkness of the evening. Mentioning my husband's name, he immediately remembered him. The protective look in his eyes and the sincere smile on his face eased my worries.

I uttered the code word, "We're leaving." He took me to a spot where no one outside could see us. He was very upset when I told him what had happened to my husband. "We had made arrangements with reliable people. It seems something went wrong," he said, and looking at my baby, he asked, "Are you going to set out with the baby?"

"What other choice do I have?"

"You're right… I wish there was another way."

I took off two of my gold bracelets and handed them to him.

"I hope these will suffice," I said.

"One is enough. Convert the rest into cash. You'll also need to give the men a thousand euros. Don't give it all at first. I'll arrange the first installment. They'll contact you soon for the details," he said.

Clearly, Mesut was also putting himself at risk. All I could say was, "May God be pleased with you."

When I returned home and hugged my sister, saying, "I'm leaving," her eyes filled with tears,

"I don't know what to say. I can't comprehend all that's happening. If you have no other choice, what else can be done?"

"Even if there might be another way, I don't know what it is," I said.

My father used to say, "There will always be difficulties. The important thing is to resist them and look for solutions." I've always agreed with my father. I'm sure he would have told me to pursue the solution if he were here now. I was determined and would not give up.

Leaving

Three days later, I received a call. The person said, "Come to this address tomorrow evening," making my entire body tense. It was all so sudden. I started to prepare. I had a good idea of what to take with me. I sold my bracelets at a jeweler's. The rent for the house was a trivial amount, so I wasn't worried. After I left, Mesut would sell the furniture and other things at home and give the money to my sister.

The following day, the phone rang early, and the voice on the other end said, "We're leaving Friday at seven." They had delayed it by two days. I reviewed the items I was taking with me. In case they fell into the river, I wrapped the money and all the clothes in plastic bags very well. I gave all my remaining clothes to my sister. Among them were items I had only worn once or twice. I wasn't sad since my sister would wear them. But I was very sad to leave my kitchen utensils behind.

My farewell was only with my sister. Both of us knew we might not see each other for many years.

On Friday, I took a taxi to the given address with my baby and a backpack. As soon as I got out of the taxi, a man in his thirties, his face barely visible under his hat and dressed to conceal his identity, approached me and said in a rushed manner, "Follow me." Clutching my baby, I followed the man. We passed three or four streets. The weight of both the baby and the backpack was starting to wear on me. Finally, at the corner of a street, he opened the door of a car with its hazard lights flashing and said, "Jump in without looking around," and then he quickly walked away.

We were on our way to Edirne. A light rain was falling. After the highway, we entered dark roads. Beside me was a family, and in front was a young man. The driver instructed, "If we get stopped, say we're going to Selimiye. Make up a story!"

No one asked, "What kind of story?" The young man sitting in the front, who was a Turkish teacher, quickly concocted a scenario. With a few adjustments, it seemed plausible to all of us. The driver's second command was, "Turn off your phones completely!" The driver was a human smuggler, and we were his cargo. Our eyes were glued to the roads.

Our concern: What if the police stopped us? What if we couldn't answer their questions? The family beside me also had a baby. The mother's lips were moving silently. She was praying. The driver's phone rang occasionally. His replies were short, "Okay... Very well... That road... Okay."

After a while, we turned off the main road. It was clear we had entered village roads. The driver reassured, "There might be checkpoints here too, but no worries. No panic."

All our questions to the driver were left unanswered. Whatever we asked, he replied, "My job is to transport you. I don't involve myself in anything else. Don't ask any more questions." We arrived at a rundown, dilapidated house. The driver quickly got out and said, "This is as far as I go. Don't turn on your phones. Don't use any flashlight. Don't go inside. Wait behind this house," and then he left.

How long would we wait?

Why would we wait?

Where would we go from here?

Why couldn't we enter the house?

It seemed we would find the answers to these swirling questions through experience. The air had cooled after the rain. The Turkish teacher said, "I'll wait here. If a car comes, I'll let you know."

We clumsily made our way to the back of the house. My baby was asleep. I almost tripped over a stone and dropped the small suitcase I was carrying. I held my baby tight. I sat down, leaning my back against the house's wall, and started breastfeeding my baby to keep him from crying.

About twenty minutes later, a car arrived at the front of the house, and five more people joined us. Among them was a child. We greeted the newcomers. Now we were three children and eight adults in total. The newly joined children were three years and four months old. My baby was two months old.

The second car also left. We had all turned off our phones. It was well past midnight. We all sat leaning against the wall of the house, waiting like sacrificial lambs.

I just stood there with my baby in my arms, observing the surroundings. What could be the story of these people whose names I didn't even know yet? Their reasons for fleeing were clear, but how much could I trust them? What if I got caught like my husband? What if these human smugglers handed us over to the gendarmerie or the police?

In the silence and darkness of the night, my thoughts clashed with one another. The Turkish teacher broke the silence, "It seems we are all on the same path." No one responded, but his words made us put aside our thoughts. Receiving no reply, he continued, "I spent nine months inside. A month after getting out, a warrant was issued for my rearrest. I didn't surrender. I've been hiding here and there for months. Now I'm here." Again, no one responded.

The three-year-old's name was Rami. Rami? A name I had never heard before. The baby's name was Fatih. I haven't mentioned the name of my baby yet, have I? It is Berat. My husband chose his name which means exoneration. Hopefully, our journey would also conclude with exoneration.

Rami's father said, "It's one o'clock. No one is around. Have they tricked us?" The Turkish teacher said, "This is how smugglers operate. They don't put themselves at risk. Everything has its time; we have no choice but to wait." And so, we did. As we waited, we slowly started sharing our stories, bit by bit.

It was my turn. I hesitated whether to share or not. After all, these were people I had just met. "I'm from Turkmenistan," I said, and they looked at me as if to ask, "What are you doing here?" "My husband is in prison. And I am here," I summarized my situation briefly.

The middle-aged couple who came in the same car with me barely spoke at all. They only shared their names and briefly mentioned they were academics, without going into detail. Maybe they weren't academics at all. Their demeanor suggested they might have had more formal jobs, perhaps as judges, prosecutors, or in some significant government position.

Fatih's parents had been teachers in Tatarstan. Both had arrest warrants issued against them. The children, perhaps bored by the adult conversation, started crying. Those of us with children moved to the other side of the house. Thankfully, it wasn't cloudy. We could see around just enough. As Fatih's mother and I breastfed our children, Rami's mother began telling a story. We, the three women, started dozing off where we sat.

The Turkish teacher's anxious voice woke us up, "Sisters, we're leaving," he said. A larger vehicle had arrived this time. Eight adults and three children squeezed into it. When we tried to ask the driver questions, he sternly said, "No one asks any questions," adding, "You'll see when we get there."

Crossing

And then Maritza appeared in the distance. The car stopped about two hundred meters from the river. The driver instructed, "You will go to the tree you see ahead. Two people will be waiting for you there. Keep your children quiet at all costs. They shouldn't cry. We mentioned sleeping aids; you brought them, right? Give them to the kids now."

Fatih's mother took out the sleep syrup and administered it to her baby with a small plastic spoon. Berat was already asleep. I dripped a few drops into his mouth too. The driver hurried us, "Hurry up, the gendarmerie patrol will pass by soon. Don't cause us any trouble," he said, and after letting us out of the car, he drove off, disappearing from sight.

We started walking towards the river. The ground was slightly muddy. The Turkish teacher took the bag from my back. The full moon had vanished. We could barely see where we were stepping. Rami's father whispered, "Everyone, recite the prayers you know. Let's keep praying until we cross the river," he said.

I began to recite the Bismillah[58] continuously. When we reached the tree, two people were waiting for us. One of them, with a broken Turkish, said, "Crouch here." We had no choice but to obey. We crouched. They inflated a boat with a device and lowered it into the river. One of the smugglers got in first, followed by me. As I stepped into the boat, my foot got wet. "Oh no, there's water here," I said, to which one smuggler calmly replied, "It's okay, no problem." The other harshly said, "Shh, don't talk."

We had no choice but to board. The river was slightly wavy. We had moved a bit when suddenly, dozens of birds flew overhead, landing on the trees across the river and started chirping. Their chirping continued until we reached the middle of the river. I shivered slightly. Fatih's mother held my hand tightly. Our children were asleep.

I looked back at the land that I knew as my country one last time. I felt such an intense sadness as if I was leaving my own homeland. Not just me, but everyone in the boat looked back with a longing. I experienced in that boat a moment that felt like hours. I had faced many farewells before, but this was different. I had left my husband behind. His smile, love, and support had always been with me, but for a moment, I felt truly getting distant from him. It was like the description of love in one of the poems of Yasemin Kayip:

We lamented our losses at times,

our desires lingering in our eyes.

As our beloved went to others in her most beautiful state,

Our souls ached more while listening to love songs.

---

58 Bismillah is one of the most important phrases in Islam and is used by Muslims mostly before starting any good deed as well as beginning of most daily actions. It means "In the name of God, the Most Gracious, the Most Merciful."

...

Our love was different, and this is why...

We couldn't love anyone else.

I was leaving everything behind, including the dreams I had built for the future, my dream of becoming a professor at a university. I was leaving my family behind, even though it was in a different country. I was on the road with the hope of a new beginning.

Before boarding the boat, the other shore seemed only fifty meters away. Apparently, it wasn't so; every ten meters felt like ten kilometers. An endless stretch of time... The human smuggler at the front pulled out a small flashlight from his pocket and flashed it twice towards the opposite shore. Soon after, a response came from the other side. It seemed we were on the right path, and the danger of being caught was behind us.

I was on the road without knowing when I would return; we all were. Swallowing our grievances, we had laid our dreams out in front of us. The truth was, a sense of peace had enveloped us all. The sound of birds was still audible. The full moon had re-emerged from behind the clouds, increasing its brightness. It was as if we were on a romantic trip, heading on a vacation. The faces of everyone in the boat showed they were immersed in the same intense emotions. The smuggler beside me, as if questioning the moon's sudden appearance, glanced at it and muttered to himself, "The gendarmes must have seen us." But he was missing something: the full moon, illuminating the night, was whispering that our future would be bright.

When we were about twenty meters from the shore, the flashlight on the other side blinked twice. The smuggler took out his phone for a brief conversation, then turned to his companion, said something in Arabic, and urgently told us, "This is marshland.

Toward downstream…" but as the boat's direction changed, the current began to drag us. The man at the front panicked, "Hold onto the branches," he said. The Turkish teacher placed his backpack on the floor of the boat and tried to grab a branch. Impossible! His hands found nothing. The other men, too, had their arms full with children and backpacks. The couple who claimed to be academics clung to each other. Images of dozens of people like us, leaving their homelands only to capsize and drown in the Maritza River or the Aegean Sea, flashed before my eyes. I held my baby tighter. The screams of a mother who had been swept away in this river with her two children a few months ago echoed in my ears. Were we going to be next? I couldn't bear to think about it. The boat was unstable. For a moment, I thought everything was about to end. Our lives, loved ones, ambitions, needs, wants…

The smuggler at the back told Rami's father, "You move slowly to the right side." There was nothing to hold onto in the rubber boat. It rocked again. The silently recited prayers became vocal. On his third attempt, the Turkish teacher grabbed a branch and started pulling it, but the branch broke off in his hand. The boat spun around once more. Rami's father was trying to change his position when he almost flipped over. Everyone in the boat tried to hold onto each other. As the boat spun, we were all shaken. It felt like a balancing act, a moment intertwined with fear and hope. If the boat capsized, I would be the weakest link. I didn't know how to swim. But at least someone might save my baby. No, I shouldn't think like that. "Hasbunallahu wa ni'mal wakeel[59]," I said firmly. A sense of peace filled me. A few others around me repeated, "Hasbunallahu wa ni'mal wakeel."

Fatih's father placed his backpack inside the boat and reached out to grab a branch. Finally, he caught a thick branch and pulled

---

59 A prayer in Arabic, in translation: "Sufficient for us is Allah, and He is the best Disposer of affairs."

it towards himself in a controlled manner. "Nobody move; I'll put my strength into this branch. Let's stay calm," he said. He clung to it as if it might uproot from the ground. The boat stabilized. It wasn't spinning or shaking anymore. As the branch was pulled into the boat, two others helped pull. Thankfully, we were about ten feet from the shore. The leading smuggler jumped out of the boat and said, "It's not a marsh after all," pulling the boat towards the shore with all his might. We all took a deep breath. We had set foot on the soil of another country!

Dawn was just beginning to break. While one man hurriedly checked the boat, the other turned to us, agitated, and said, "We need to leave. Give us the remaining money!" Everyone had wrapped their money in plastic bags and taped them tightly, just as I had. We handed the money to the men. They pocketed it without counting. When the Turkish teacher asked, "Aren't you going to count the money?" The smuggler grinned, "No need. We trust you won't short us," and they quickly disappeared as they had arrived on the boat. We understood whom the man referred to with the word "you," but I still wished he had elaborated on it. After distancing about fifty feet further, they waved at us again.

We all found a dry spot and sat down. We looked at each other meaningfully. We had succeeded. There was no one in sight. We felt somewhat safe but wondered where we would go next. The effects of the sleeping pills must have worn off because the children began to wake up one by one. Fatih's mother and I separated from the group, moved a bit further away, and squatted down to breastfeed our children. However, we were soon attacked by mosquitoes. Fatih's mother was prepared; she took out insect repellent from her bag and sprayed it on our hands after we finished breastfeeding.

Fatih's father said, "We need to move quickly. Let's get going," prompting everyone to stand up. We started walking without a specific direction, meandering along the edges of fields. Where were the people with whom the smugglers had communicated using flashlights while crossing the river? There was no one around. Now, we had only one goal: to find a road with passing cars and apply for asylum at the first police station we encountered.

The rising sun, the earth we stepped on with our wet and muddy feet, the sounds of chirping birds, the branches swaying in the light wind seemed different somehow. Even though we didn't know what awaited us a mile ahead, we believed they wouldn't arrest and imprison us. The freedom we felt made nature communicate with us differently.

The Turkish teacher kindly carried my backpack again. The questions asked by three-year-old Rami's parents seemed to echo in my mind as well.

"Dad, where are we?"

"Why are we here?"

"Mom, I'm hungry, isn't there any food?"

"Mom, I'm thirsty."

"Dad, my feet are so wet."

"Ugh, I'm tired."

...

Finally, the cultivated fields ended. We sat down under a tree. Our shoes, socks, and even our clothes were covered in mud. Some of us changed into spare socks they had in their backpacks. Those who had food in their bags took out whatever they had. Crackers, biscuits, nuts… We snacked a little. When I asked, "Can I turn on my phone?" Fatih's father replied, "Right… There shouldn't be any problem here anymore." We unwrapped our phones from the tightly sealed plastic bags. The only person I could call was my sister. It was as if my sister was waiting by the phone because she picked up immediately. "Sister, we've crossed," I said. She responded, "Thank God," and we hung up. We had agreed to do so before the journey.

After walking on footpaths for about an hour, we finally reached the main road. I had never walked such a distance in my life. I felt blisters forming on my feet. Cars passed by, some honking their horns, whether as a reaction or a warning, we couldn't tell. Eventually, a vehicle stopped beside us, and the driver asked in broken Turkish,

"Need police?" As if we had agreed on it, we all responded in unison,

"No, thank you."

We wanted to go directly to a police station to surrender ourselves.

After a while, another vehicle stopped. The driver leaned towards us and asked in English,

"Are you escaping from Erdoğan?" We understood English well enough, but no one responded.

I thought to myself, "Yes, we are escaping from his curse."

Considering we were a large group with children, drawing too much attention, we decided to split up and walk in groups of three. I continued walking with Fatih's family. Eventually, a town came into view. We still hadn't come across a police station. We were exhausted. It was nearing noon. At the entrance of the town, we moved to the side of a dilapidated house where Fatih's mother and I began to breastfeed our babies. The Turkish teacher left the group intending to buy food and drinks. While breastfeeding my baby, I fell into a brief sleep. When I opened my eyes, two men in official uniforms were standing in front of me. They were police officers. Turning to my side, I saw that Fatih's mother had also fallen asleep. At that moment, the Turkish teacher returned with drinks and ice cream in hand. In a moment of confusion, he offered what he had brought to the police.

After greeting us, the officers said, "Let's go," and we gathered our things. They loaded us into a transporter-style vehicle. Inside the car, a surprise awaited us. Our companions from the journey were also there. Upon arriving at the police station, the first question from the chief officer was, "Are you hungry? Do your children need anything?"

Five Months **Later**

I am writing these lines from a house where I live with three other women friends. I am in Thessaloniki. It has been precisely five months since we crossed the border into Greece. Before arriving here, I experienced life in two different camps. By camp, I mean a refugee camp, somewhat akin to a prison.

The officers at the police station meticulously took our records and listened to our stories before transferring us to the first camp center. It was a camp with dark and crowded dormitories, holding Syrians, Afghans, Africans, Pakistanis, and people from various other places. The dorms had bunk beds, trash strewn about the floors, people blaring noisy music, shouting to understand each other, sharing a dirty bed between two, filthy toilets and bathrooms... My only consolation was being in the same dorm with baby Fatih and his mother.

We had not been in the camp for four days when a camp official took me to an office where a police officer was present. The officer said, "You are not Turkish. Your case is different. You will go to another camp." I responded instinctively, "What do you mean? I am thoroughly Turkish. My home country may be different, but our experiences are the same." The officer seemed unconvinced by my words, "You are a citizen of another country. What problem do you have with Erdoğan? Most of the arrivals claim to be from the Hizmet Movement. What is your connection?"

They hadn't asked me so many questions at the police station. "Hizmet has no race. It's a service to humanity and is not unique to a nationality or country to help those in need, to dedicate oneself to education. Besides, I am married to a Turkish citizen. He is now in prison in Turkey." I listed everything that came to mind to the officer.

After speaking on the phone in Greek with someone, the officer said, "You will have to wait until tomorrow. You can explain your situation to the person in charge of refugees," and he decided against sending me somewhere else.

I couldn't sleep that night. It wasn't just because of the dirty smell of the bed, pillow, and blanket, but also the noise from people coming and going into the dorm at all hours was making it impossible to sleep. The next day, I met with the person in charge of refugees. He said similar things like the police. He explained that I was brought to this camp by mistake, and that I actually shouldn't have been kept here. I had no choice. I had to go to another camp with Berat, inevitably separating from Fatih's mother.

In the new camp, containers were lined up in a row. My baby and I were squeezed next to a Syrian family with three children. It wasn't very clean here either, but at least there was a bed where I could sleep more comfortably side by side with my baby. Thankfully, they provided a new bedding set, clean towels, diapers, and shampoo here. There was also internet access for four hours in the evening. However, there was so much noise that Berat's sleep schedule was disrupted. Sometimes his crying wouldn't stop. Just as I was beginning to get accustomed to the conditions on the fifth day, they told me that I would be relocated to another camp once again. It was a challenging adjustment, but I knew I had to adapt quickly. We were put in an open vehicle with two long benches inside. There were two more families inside. I hoped I was moving to a better place, but that wasn't the case. They sent me back to the first camp.

They placed me in a room similar to a prison dormitory, with women from different nationalities inside. Most were single. There were also families with children. I was overwhelmed by the crowd, the loud conversations, the blaring music. There was no order. I hadn't cried this much, not during the police raids, not when I was separated from my husband and sister, not even while crossing the Maritza. I had always tried to stay strong. But this camp life was suffocating me. I couldn't hold back my tears. The Afghans had been in the same place for two months. How much longer would I be here? This camp didn't have internet access; phone calls were made by loading credit onto phones.

I visited the camp administration numerous times, pleading, "I can't bear this anymore." The staff tried to console me, but I was out of strength.

My friends from the camp had left for Thessaloniki. The only ones I hadn't heard from were the couple who never really revealed much about themselves. I called Fatih's mother. With the help of friends, they had found a place to live. She said if I could leave the camp, there was a house where women stayed, and I could settle there too. But how would I get out?

I also called the Turkish teacher. He had found a place to stay with other single individuals.

"Sister, there's a lawyer here known to our friends. Let's talk to him, but he's on a trip now to another country. As soon as he returns, we'll get in touch," he said.

I felt a bit relieved but wondered if I could last until then.

A week passed, and I was still living with three Afghan women. Unable to receive any news by the seventh day, I called my sister in the middle of the night, barely knowing what I was saying, "Notify the furniture dealer, let those men take me back. I want to return to Turkey. Even if they imprison me," I said. My sister informed me that they had sold the household items and she was on a bus to the airport. She continued, urging me to hold on, saying, "Every darkness has its dawn." They were simple words of consolation, but they comforted me. I didn't want to upset her further, telling her I might move to a house soon. I adamantly told her not to inform our sick father or mother about my situation.

I called my mother-in-law. Before I could say anything, she said, "The police came looking for you. Where are you?" She didn't ask about her grandchild or how I was doing. They had only visited my husband in prison once, citing living in a different city as their excuse. I replied, "I'm fine. It's normal for the police to come. Don't worry. I can take care of myself," and hung up.

How was someone feeling utterly alone and at the bottom of a well supposed to fend for themselves? Sometimes, I found myself drowning in endless darkness.

It was Friday. I felt all my escape routes had closed. All hope was lost. I held Berat close to my chest, reciting all the prayers I knew. I was on the verge of losing myself when the voice of a camp official calling my name snapped me back to reality. I quickly gathered myself and went to the camp administration office. The official said in English, "You are free now," filling me with joy and disbelief, "Are you serious? You are not kidding, right?" I asked.

It wasn't a joke. I was free. Without hesitating, I packed my belongings. I called Fatih's mother, who explained how to get to Thessaloniki.

Thankfully, I had enough money to manage for a while, having exchanged my gold jewelry for Euros in Turkey. I took a taxi to the bus station and arrived in Thessaloniki on the first bus.

Five months have passed since my arrival in Thessaloniki. Here there are more than five friends like me who have left their spouses behind in Turkey. We live in two groups in different houses. Each has their own story.

To summarize the situation since the crossing: My father became quite distressed when he learned of my arrival in Greece. He felt relieved knowing I was happy where I stayed. We continue to speak on the phone weekly. My in-laws also found out about my crossing to Greece but made no comments. I tried to send messages to my husband through a lawyer. When the lawyer said I could write letters, I began sending them every fifteen days. The lawyer assures me he's delivering them. Maybe one day, I'll receive a reply!

The rights granted to asylum seekers in Greece are quite limited. Moreover, the country's severe economic crisis pushes many to attempt to move to other European countries. But these aren't simple journeys; they're complicated beyond words. The Turkish teacher who arrived on the same boat has somehow made it to Germany. The struggle for others to go to other countries in Europe continues, often ending in disappointment, but we have no other choice!

I've attempted to go to Germany twice, but due to several setbacks, I had to return. I'll try again in two weeks.

God is generous!

Thessaloniki, 2018

We would like to thank everyone who has contributed to this book.

*Our sole wish is that the injustice, lawlessness,
and victimization that many people in Turkey
have been suffering from, will come to an end as soon as possible
via the re-establishment of the rule of law.*

EDITED BY
HAFZA GİRDAP

SESSİZ ÇIĞLIK
Türkiye'deki Zulmün Gerçek Hikayeleri
Mina Leyla

UMUT HİKAYELERİ
Mülteci ve Öteki Çocukların Kalemiyle
Editör Doğan Yücel

THE HEAVENLY TEACHER MURDERED IN PRISON
Halime Gülsu
Zeynep Kayadelen

MINA LEYLA
ÇALINMIŞ HAYATLAR
YENİ TÜRKİYE'NİN HİKAYESİ

STORIES OF HOPE
Written by Children
Refugee and Oppressed
Edited by Doğan Yücel

Nasıl Öldürüldüm
Halime Gülsu'nun Hayatı
Zeynep Kayadelen

BROKEN LIVES
STORIES FROM NEW TURKEY
MINA LEYLA
EDITED BY SAIT ONAL

THE LIFE AND LEGACY OF
GÖKHAN AÇIKKOLLU
A TEACHER TORTURED TO DEATH
Mina Leyla

JUSTICE DELAYED IS JUSTICE DENIED
M. Ertuğrul İncekul
Translated by
Ömer Akbury

AST PUBLISHING

Backdrop of the PakTurk Schools Crisis in Pakistan
The Ordeals of the Turkish Teachers
DREAMS
INTERRUPTED
Engin Yiğit

SUSMAYAN
Hatıralar
Mehmet
Akpak

Murder of Halil Dinc
in
Slow Motion
as told by his wife
Nihayet Dinc
Zeynep
Kayadelen

Gülerek Geçtim
Dünyadan
Eşi Nihayet Dinç'in anlatımıyla
Öğretmen
Halil DİNÇ'in Hayatı
Zeynep
Kayadelen

Öğretmen Gökhan
Açıkkollu
Bir Şehadet Bestesi
Mina Leyla
Eşi Tülay Açıkkollu'nun anlatımıyla

FRAGILE PATHS, STRONG HEARTS:
Stories of
Rebirth
MEHMET AKPAK

JOURNEY

YOLCULUK

IF YOU WOULD LIKE TO SUPPORT OUR BOOK PUBLISHING EFFORTS

☑ CREDIT CARD OR DEBIT

silencedturkey.org/donatenow

☑ PAYPAL

paypal.me/ast111

☑ ZELLE

advocatesofsilencedturkey@gmail.com

☑ PATREON

patreon.com/advocatesofsilencedturkey

9 798328 225403